Speak,
A Black Man's View of America
ROLAND S. MARTIN

Advance praise for Speak, Brother!
A Black Man's View of America

"More than almost any writer I've known, black or white, Roland Martin has the knack of cutting through the noise to get to the truth, sometimes a painful truth, but the truth nonetheless. This is Martin at his in-your-face best. Whether he's roasting the mainstream media for its lack of diversity, Puff Daddy and Destiny's Child for their spiritual hypocrisy, or Charles Barkley for his portrait in chains, Martin is right on, a voice that cannot be ignored."

Tim Madigan, author, The Burning: Massacre, Destruction, and the Tulsa Race Riot of 1921

"Roland S. Martin's voice is powerful, poignant and spiritual. He expertly captures the pain, passion, and possibilities for African Americans, especially African American men, in the so-called 'post-racial' twenty-first century. Martin is a DuBois-style 'race man,' a King-style preacher-critic, and a journalist who can sling opinions with the best of the pundits. He combines these elements to present his uniquely compelling voice in presenting this utterly essential view of America. This is a fascinating read."

Dr. Julianne Malveaux, economist and author

"Roland will not let you down. He will rile, inspire and provoke you. He will make you laugh, scream and thrust your fist into the air (or through the pages of the book). He will teach and he will tantalize. And all of this could happen before you reach the second paragraph! Roland S. Martin is a smart and passionate new voice who speaks for thousands of young black men coming of age in the new millennium."

Roy Johnson, editor-in-chief, Savoy Magazine

"Roland Martin is a voice of reason, rage and unwavering blackness. He is a 21st century 'race man,' cut for the same mold that produced the angry voices of the 1920s Harlem Renaissance and the 1960s Black Power Movement."

DeWayne Wickham, columnist, USA Today and Gannett News Service

"Most people hold back because they are concerned about offending somebody. Roland Martin just don't care. And that's a good thing."

Reginald Hudlin, filmmaker, Boomerang, House Party

"Roland S. Martin refuses to be compromised by anyone. He is true to himself and to our race. Keep the truth coming."

Zina Garrison, former tennis star

"Roland's perspective on news stories, his ability to get to the heart of the matter and his insight into issues that are of interest to African Americans are all reasons that I enjoy his writings."

Tom Joyner, host, ABC Radio Network's nationally syndicated Tom Joyner Morning Show

"The mixture of truth presented in a brash sometime raw point of view by Roland Martin often brings a reader face-to-face with the fundamental issues on the minds of Black Americans across this country. Fearless in his approach, Martin does his homework and tackles topics that have earned him respect but attracted some critics. He can be described as bombastic, compassionate, outspoken, candid and sincere – the true reflection of a journalist who cares."

Sonceria (Sonny) Messiah-Jiles, publisher, Houston Defender, Houston's leading black newspaper

"A Roland Martin commentary is a shot across the bow of our collective senses. Whether he's opining about the sticky issue of race relations, the complicated morass of men and women relationships or the state of the American family, Roland is always provocatively incisive. His commentaries, more often than not, hit us right between the eyes and shatters our assumptions."

James Campbell, editorial writer, Houston Chronicle

"Read him, and you'll come to know and respect Roland Martin, the plainspoken citizen of George Bush's Texas and Roland Martin, the insightful journalist/commentator. But if you try and pigeonhole Martin into a predictable niche, you will be met with certain disappointment and frustration. His style defies easy definition. It is frank, provocative and intellectually honest, delivered with passion, fervor and no-holds-barred candor. Over the years, I've witnessed his maturity and growth. But he has a refreshing youthful brashness about him that's unchangeable."

Kenneth F. Bunting, executive editor, Seattle Post-Intelligencer

"Roland Martin has worked in the news business...so naturally he has eyes and ears everywhere. He can smell the story before we see it. Fortunately, he uses his power for good-exposing corruption, pointing out inconsistencies, holding the mirror up to our black faces. Every black American should read, *Speak, Brother!* You will inevitably come away with another way of seeing yourself."

Yolanda Young, author, On Our Way to Beautiful, A Family Memoir

"Be sure to fasten your seat belts. *Speak, Brother! A Black Man's View of America* is an insightfully irreverent glimpse into the often-silenced thoughts of today's black man. It doesn't pause for thoughts or stop for signs. It's full speed ahead!"

Tracie Howard, co-author, Revenge Is Best Served Cold

"Roland Martin offers a provocative, no-holds barred viewpoint on the issues of the day. His is a rising voice of commentary for black America."

Valorie Burton, author, Rich Minds, Rich Rewards: 52 Ways to Enhance, Enrich and Empower Your Life

"Roland Martin is a dynamic journalist with a 'take-no-prisoners' attitude that's refreshing! Informative, entertaining, committed and connected, Roland's missives are not to be missed."

Paula Walker, KNBC President/General Manager; NBC Senior Vice President of Diversity

"Edgy, engaging and thought-provoking are just a few of the words which describe the writings of Roland Martin. Martin is more than just 'a Black man in America.' He is a powerful voice challenging the stereotypes about Black and White America and the old models that have defined a generation. He is insightful and yet demanding in his prescriptions for confronting what's at stake for all of us. He is passionate and unafraid. He is an ideal commentator on our times."

Michael Steele, Chairman, Maryland Republican Party

"Roland S. Martin is one of the brightest young leaders on the scene today. With his reporting, he goes to the heart of the matter. In his commentary, he does not pull punches. In his speeches, he has some tantalizing observations."

David R. Squires, Editor, BlackVoices.com/BVQ magazine

Reader praise for Speak, Brother!
A Black Man's View of America

"I thank God for a level-headed person like yourself."

Jacqueline Hayes, Chicago

"It's very refreshing to have someone like yourself to stand up for Black interests in the present climate."

T. Henry Hale Jr., Fairfax, Virginia

"You always come through with a rather good point in a lot of situations in which we find negative."

Johnette Leday, Beaumont, Texas

"You have a writing gift from God. Your work is easy on the mind and flows like a bubbling stream. I appreciate your ability to communicate the English language. Your heart is in all the right places and…you can never go wrong when you are turning over new ideas (every end is always a beginning) without a hidden agenda. And that my brother separates you from the pack."

Stephen Giles, Dallas

"I am grateful that we have your media voice to speak over the negative voices that are so prominently thrust into the media forefront."

Renee Williams Jefferson, Olympia Fields, Illinois

"That was an awesome article!!!!!!!!!!!!!!!!!!!!!"

Monica Greer, Brownsville, Tennessee

"Fantastic comments. You brought tears to my eyes."

Karen Clayton, Houston

Roland, your piece/assessment of the Halle/Denzel/Oscar debate gave me chills..."

Sandra Varner, Atlanta

"Let me start by saying I am not a fan of anyone. I don't believe in being a fan. I think you are slowly changing my 'fan theory.' I have to say that your commentaries are very enlightening. They make me think in a way that I have never thought before and about things that I thought I knew about; I consider myself pretty enlightened. So let me say to you keep up the good work and keep informing our people."

Jackie Clemons, Cincinnati

"I really appreciate the eye-opening editorial."

Josie Kite, Greensboro, North Carolina

"All I can say is OUCH! You just touched me. Thank you for this article."

Twanda Sweet, Houston

"I just read your commentary and I must say that you are right on it."

Vance R. Kenney, Gary, Indiana

"Thanks for the wake up call."

Leslie Lee, Kansas City, Kansas

"I just wanted to send you a little note and let you know how glad I am that you wrote this article. It was truly an eye opener for me."

Shatara Hester, Grand Rapids, Michigan

"I look forward to more of your intense thoughts and words. Thank you. I speak for all my girls when I say thank you for 'keeping it real.'"

Ingrid Brewster, San Antonio, Texas

Speak, Brother!

A Black Man's View of America

ROLAND S. MARTIN

R. Martin Media Group
www.rolandsmartin.com

Martin, Roland S.
Speak, Brother! A Black Man's View of America.
Roland S. Martin – 1st edition
Published by R. Martin Media Group

ISBN 0-9719107-0-7

Cover design by Frank Gonzales, www.gonzographix.com; Brandon Green,
www.revelationmedia.com
Cover photo by Jesse Hornbuckle, www.hornbucklephoto.com

Printed in the United States of America

DEDICATION

To God for ordering my steps in His word and for picking me up when I was down. To my beloved wife, the Rev. Jacquie C. Hood Martin, who is truly an anointed woman and is undoubtedly God-sent. Thank you, thank you, thank you for all your prayers and support. And to my parents, Reginald and Emelda Martin, who encouraged me not be shy about speaking my mind, even when it wasn't popular. They are also to be commended for producing five jewels: Reginald Jr., Roland, Levita, Kenya and Zina.

Speak, Brother!
A Black Man's View of America

TABLE OF CONTENTS

TABLE OF CONTENTS

Speak, Brother!
ACKNOWLEDGEMENTS

During my time at Texas A&M University, my dad asked me why I was going into journalism. With an incredulous look on my face, I replied, "What in the world were you thinking? We had to watch news five hours a day. Did you not think one of us was going into the media?"

A smile came across his face, and I always get a huge laugh when telling others that story. It seems as if journalism has been in my blood from my elementary and middle school days. So common sense says when Jack Yates High School came calling about its Magnet School of Communications in 1983, my choice was fairly simple.

A huge thanks must go to teachers and staff at the school who trained me in the fine arts of communications, including Mary Waites, Thelma Houston and Otho Raye White. During that period wonderful African American journalists like Charles Williams, now at WCBS in New York, Felicia Jeter, and Alma Newsome came in and out of our classroom, sharing their stories in the industry and providing an enlightening view of this business.

Those connections and dialogues helped when I left for Texas A&M in 1987. One of the first people I met was the department head, Dr. Douglas Starr. To this date, Dr. Starr is still teaching at the university, even at the age of 77. With his energy and wonderful stories of covering the Civil Rights Movement, Dr. Starr has been an inspiration and a wealth of knowledge for so many of us who were honored to be in his presence. Others to thank include Bob Rogers, an irascible and tough editor who could whip us with his pencil, but who taught us while doing it. Dr. Don Tomlinson also was solid in teaching about ethics and the law, and most of all, he cared while doing it.

Learning about this business is one thing but doing it is another. I could have had an internship with CBS News in Dallas in 1989, but I turned it down to work for the *Houston Defender*, Houston's leading Black newspaper. Under the direction of publisher/owner Sonceria (Sonny) Messiah-Jiles and editor Marilyn Marshall, I was allowed the chance to cover major newsmakers, write editorials and do some wonderful and exciting things. Some have complained about the black press and said it's irrelevant. I will never say that because were it not for the black press, I would not have had a chance to flourish. Thanks also go to Jim Washington, who gave me the flexibility to run the shop as I saw fit as managing editor of the *Dallas Weekly*.

Robert Borden, the editorial page editor of the *Bryan-College Station Eagle*, deserves some praise for the columns I have written over the years. When others looked at him like he was nuts for allowing a 19-year-old to write columns, Borden didn't care. If it was good and compelling, he would run it. Thanks Bob, for giving a brother a chance and allowing talent, and not race or youth, to rule the day.

Speak, Brother!

There is no organization that could get as much credit for my development and ascension in this business than the National Association of Black Journalists. From the moment I joined the board of directors of NABJ in 1989, my life and career has blossomed beyond what I expected.

I cannot name everyone who has touched and affected me one way or another, but there are a few who must be given their props: Sheila and Rodney Brooks; Paula Walker Madison; Vernon Jarrett; Ray Metoyer and Angela Robinson; David Squires; Drew Berry; Michael Fountain; Greg Moore; Rochelle Riley; Betty Baye; Vanessa Williams; Sheila Smoot; the late Charles Jackson; and Callie Crossley.

Let me thank the co-workers who I have had a chance to work alongside over the years at the *Austin American-Statesman*, the *Fort Worth Star-Telegram*, KKDA-AM the *Dallas Weekly*, *Houston Defender*, BlackAmericaWeb.com and *Savoy* Magazine.

Speaking of *Savoy*, special thanks is extended to Roy Johnson, who God gave the vision of the magazine and who has done a stellar job of making it a reality as editor-in-chief, as well as editorial director of Vanguarde Media. My friendship with Roy goes back years to NABJ, and I can't thank him for extending me the invitation to join the staff when it launched, as well as our personal friendship. My golf partner is also a loving husband and father, and I can't say enough about his wife, Barbara, and children Edwyn and Missy. Thanks for letting me bunk at your house when I'm in New York!

Other friends who must be shown much love include all the brothers of Alpha Phi Alpha Fraternity, Inc., Pi Omicron chapter, Texas A&M University; Michael and Donna Williams, Roger B. Brown, Denise Mitchem, Anthony "Spud" Webb and Matthew Harden Jr. Thank you John Ware for your advice, encouragement and counsel.

Sherilyn Smith deserves recognition. She is a former co-worker who has a caring and giving heart and who can be counted on. Thanks for picking up my mail when I'm traveling, checking on the house and depositing money in my bank accounts and swooping me up on a moment's notice from the airport! Sherilyn, you are a doll. Jim, give her a raise! ☺

Neil Foote is also a longtime friend from my NABJ days. Neil and I served on the NABJ board of directors and stayed in contact over the years. Who knew that he would one day be the chief operating officer of BlackAmericaWeb.com and would seek me out to run its editorial operation. You da man, Little Archie! (inside joke, folks.)

Props are also extended to Tom Joyner, the hardest working man in radio. Tom, thanks for giving me the freedom to thrive and do what I do best. Keep on enlightening and entertaining us!

A special thanks goes out to Marc Watts. I first met Marc when I was awarded an Alpha Phi Alpha Fraternity, Inc., scholarship as a high school senior. Marc gave the keynote address and we had a chance to talk that night

Speak, Brother!

in 1987. Through NABJ, we crossed paths and it was always a pleasure to hook up with him. Only God knew that, years later Marc, founder of Signature Management Group in Chicago, would become my television agent and provide the financing to make this book a reality. He is a man of his word and a solid bruh. Thanks, '06!

A huge thanks goes out to Valorie Burton (buy her book, *Rich Minds, Rich Rewards*, at www.valorieburton.com) for assisting me in the physical portion of production this book. She was a great resource in all of this. And Vickie Goble of Great Impressions is to be commended for her patience and willingness in assisting with the printing of *Speak, Brother!* I will be back.

Finally, I would be crazy if I didn't recognize the men and women who God has entrusted with being vessels in helping to build his kingdom. The Rev. Ralph D. West Sr., founder and senior pastor of Brookhollow Baptist Church (The Church Without Walls) in Houston, Texas, and the Rev. Frederick D. Haynes III, senior pastor of Friendship-West Baptist Church in Dallas, Texas, have been the men of God who have provided the spiritual insight that has made me a better man. Their sermons are truly words that come from God. Bishop Eddie L. Long of New Birth Missionary Baptist Church, thanks for keeping it real and continuing to emphasize the need for Godly men and Godly relationships. Prophetess Edna Johnson-Sneed is given much love for her friendship and stern spiritual conversations. I love her dearly for being there through the good times and the bad times.

Roland S. Martin
May 11, 2002
Cedar Hill, Texas

Speak, Brother!
FOREWORD

Offering a post-Civil Rights perspective that taps into the wellspring of today's African-American community, Roland Martin is a contemporary journalist who tells it like it is.

Unafraid to get in the faces of the powers-that-be, Martin offers his provocative commentary to those who would hear it and nod emphatically, and to those who would disagree.

An award-winning journalist who has covered everything from the 1995 bombing of the Oklahoma federal building to the intricacies of city government, Martin has worked at some of the nation's most outstanding publications: the *Fort Worth Star-Telegram*, the *Austin American-Statesman*, the *Dallas Weekly,* the *Houston Defender*, and Savoy Magazine, to name a few.

He's covered the Republican and Democratic national conventions and he's covered city hall and county government. He's interviewed and dialogued with the likes of presidents, senators, prime ministers, and the elite of the black world, including the Rev. Jesse Jackson Sr., Dr. Cornel West, Tiger Woods, Ambassador Andrew Young, Kirk Franklin and Michael Jordan.

But whether reporting the impact of inequitable government policies on black lives or covering the destruction resulting from black-on-black crime, his journalistic experience and insight into the African-American agenda gives voice to a community that is often voiceless.

Martin doesn't just sit behind a desk and pontificate on the issues of the day. He makes the effort to hit the streets and speak with all involved to present a thoughtful assessment of the news.

His candid shoot-from-the hip posture and passionate perspective are welcome antidotes in an era of increasing conservatism and shrinking diversity, where news is frequently pre-packaged and the opinions of pundits canned.

Martin's take-no-prisoners commentary may not win him friends among the newsmakers and elite of our nation, but I suspect he's already got his share of supporters among thousands of ordinary African-American men and women who share much of his opinions. Roland Martin speaks truth to power.

After reading *Speak, Brother! A Black Man's View of America* you might be inspired to open up, speak out and make yourself heard.

Hugh Price
President/CEO
National Urban League
May 2002
New York City, New York

SECTION ONE
SOCIAL CHANGE

Black America's (unrealistic) expectations for the Black CEO

March 20, 2002

African Americans may be head coaches in the NFL, quarterback teams to the Super Bowl, run their own record labels or sit across the table from world leaders, but we are still mesmerized and challenged by the view of someone black as chief executive officer of a major American corporation.

There are a number of fiefdoms and exclusive clubs in this country – the United States Senate, the White House and a number of all-white country clubs - but nowhere is there more of a gap than in the corner office of major U.S. companies.

Of the top 500 companies, as ranked by *Fortune* Magazine, only three have an African American sitting at the helm: Richard Parsons at AOL Time Warner, Kenneth Chenault at American Express and Franklin Raines of Fannie Mae. By 2004, they will likely be joined by Stanley O'Neal, who is in line to be the next CEO of Wall Street behemoth Merrill Lynch.

Their talents are immense and they are considered some of the brightest and imaginative minds in the country, but what should Black America's expectation be from these top dogs?

It is a question that is difficult to answer because much of it lies in what we are seeking.

For years the dearth of mainstream America's acknowledgement of black success has led to anger and downright enmity between African Americans and decision makers. It used to be that when the NFL draft came around black folks were up in arms over college quarterbacks being converted to wide receiver or defensive back, even as lesser talented white signal callers were given a shot to play the position. We scoffed at Major League Baseball continuing to pass over talented black coaches and former players for retread white candidates who didn't cut it in their last job. And there is lingering anger over middle and upper level African Americans who ended up training the people who eventually became their boss. America is called the land of opportunity, but when it comes to the black man and woman, historically, that has been a dream deferred.

Yet all of that is changing as opportunities are extended, not because of skin color but because of sheer talent. As a result, the chance to be considered an equal with our peers and prove our worth is being borne out each passing day.

But just as with every other "first" by an African American, a significant amount of pressure is brought to bear on these individuals. No matter how much Tiger Woods accomplishes, he will never be black enough. Michael Jordan may be the world's most famous athlete (next to Muhammad Ali), yet he is often taken to task for not speaking out enough on a variety of issues. When a black man or woman gets the chance to be the first person of color in

Speak, Brother!

the mayor's office, the expectations are so great that no one short of Martin Luther King Jr. can prove to some black folks that they are doing enough (and keep in mind, even Brother King was taken to task for not doing enough for the "black cause").

The same holds true for those black corporate executives who "have made it."

We hold such lofty ideals because of their advancement, but even they can't do it all. Their position leads many to write letters seeking money for themselves or their organization; speaking engagements come in by the truckload; and everyone wants to send their resume to the CEO for a job.

Maybe the problem stems from the fact that we have grown accustomed to "our leaders" demanding action from the streets and not the ultimate street – Wall Street.

"We have to realize these are business people," says Hugh Price, CEO of the National Urban League. "These are not civil rights people. They have devoted themselves entirely to their careers. Breaking through these areas of American life was the whole point of the Civil Rights Movement. And heaven knows we need more and more corporate leaders in this country. When you think about the resources they preside over...that's what the whole point of the movement was – penetrate all of the sector's of American life and show that we can compete with everyone else."

This is not to say that a black CEO doesn't need to give back to the community. He or she must do so, and that includes paving the way for the next generation. There is nothing worse than closing the door on someone else when it was left ajar for you. But there should be an understanding by the African American community as to what and how much is owed. And the reality is we can't place a figure on it and easily define what it is. It is unspeakable and undetermined, and can only be settled by the innermost feelings of the individual themselves.

"There are always lofty expectations when you attain that high visibility," Price said. "(Parsons, Chenault, Raines and O'Neal) do have a consciousness. Frank Raines is on the NUL board. Stanley O'Neal is on the board...the thing we have to realize is that in order for those folks to climb to those heights they've got to give those jobs 175 percent. You can't get to the top and hold on there by allowing for a whole lot of other things to intrude on your time. These folks have done quite well and they know what they are about, and as they settle in and business settles down, they can give back even more."

As *Savoy* Magazine editor-in-chief Roy Johnson puts it, maybe what we should glean the most from the appointment of a Parsons and a Chenault is not a direct benefit, but the fact that "no young black child in America has to listen to anyone who tells them they simply can't aspire to be CEO of the biggest companies in the world."

Speak, Brother!

The current and future black CEO's can't be all things to all people. What we must hope for is that they have a conscious that allows them to provide special insight to the difficulties that are put in the path of black professionals and give them a shot at maximizing their talent because of their skills.

Maybe by then the issues over how much is owed to Black America won't even be discussed because they can simply say, "Paid in Full."

As two young people lie dead, the answer appears in the mirror

May 29, 1994

As we buried our fraternity brother Reginald Broadus yesterday, nearly 250 miles away another one of our brothers was making final preparations for the most wonderful day of his life: his wedding.

Yet none of us was there to share in his jubilation.

The same goes for his bride, a member of Alpha Kappa Alpha sorority, whose sisters gathered in Beaumont to lay to rest one of their own, Crystal Miller.

It goes without saying that we would rather have been in Houston throwing rice, eating cake and serenading the happy couple with our fraternity hymn rather than singing a somber fraternity song around Reginald's flower-ladened casket.

But death doesn't ask us for our opinion. It only leaves us to deal with the consequences.

Both Reginald and Crystal, two 21-year-old honors students at Texas A&M University, were shot in the head in an apparent robbery in Dallas.

We don't know for sure what happened between the last time they were seen in the parking lot of a frat get-together at an apartment in Dallas' Red Bird area and early Monday morning, when their bodies were found three miles away off the side of a road in DeSoto.

When I checked my answering machine at 1 a.m. Tuesday and heard my Alpha Phi Alpha Fraternity brother Leon Brumfield tell me that Reginald, our past chapter president, had been murdered, I could not cry.

I could only say damn over and over.

My frat brothers, the Texas A&M student body and many others will no longer enjoy Reginald's company, see the young man with those big, wide eyes who lusted after life and had a special kinship with God.

We also could no longer feel the warm hugs and sweet hellos that Crystal distributed to friends, sorority sisters and strangers who quickly became friends.

I will never forget meeting her. She would always smile and hug my frat brother, Carlos Mitchell, and me before and after we emerged from one of our classes on Mondays, Wednesdays and Fridays. There was no special reason for the hugs; she was simply that way.

So here we are, grasping at memories of those fleeting moments that we oh-so-casually dismissed, trying to remember the brief times we shared with Reginald and Crystal, as their families and friends all scream in anger: "Why, God? Why?"

Speak, Brother!

Reginald, a psychology major, had just returned from a school-sponsored trip in London and had received only this past semester the highest award any student at Texas A&M could receive, the Buck Weirus Spirit Award.

A handful of students are given the award and its coveted Weirus watch each year as a way of thanking those students who excelled in leadership positions and had a lasting impact on the university and its 12th Man student body.

If only you could have met him. Reginald never got into confrontations or arguments. He sat back, waited until the dust settled and steered our young fraternity chapter in the right direction.

Crystal was an accounting major on an academic scholarship. She was an honors student, a member of Alpha Kappa Alpha sorority and a future business leader. Going into her senior years, her eyes were already set on a master's degree.

But all that was erased when their lives, and the babies of two mother and two fathers, were taken away.

Reginald and Crystal will never walk across the stage and accept that Aggie degree with their families applauding, screaming and crying in that ol' barn, G. Rollie White Coliseum. They will no longer go to midnight yell practices, cheer at another Aggie victory or showcase the coveted Aggie ring.

My fraternity brothers will no longer be able to lock pinkie fingers with Reginald as we sing in harmony our fraternity song. Crystal will no longer walk across the tree-lined A&M campus in her sorority's pink and green.

And many African-American children have lost two role models who shared their time and energy in the A&M area.

Reginald and Crystal are not the first and certainly not the last innocent people to be killed on this nation's streets.

And as a reporter, I have grown accustomed to distancing myself from such terrible stories. Yet in the past few months that has become harder as I watch in horror as my generation kills itself off.

I was moved nearly to tears as I stood in the sanctuary of a Como church in February during the funeral for one of three young African-American men cut down in a burst of bullets. I didn't want to go, but it was a Saturday and I was working. My anger and resentment grew throughout the tearful service and burial because three of *our children* were killed on a street corner on a warm, sunny day. And they were buried nearly a week later – side by side – on another warm, sunny day.

I hid my frustration in my notepad and tape recorder.

But I can't take it anymore.

I can't stand to see Reginald's and Crystal's families weep among friends and loved ones because their beloved children, whom they protected as best they could, were torn violently from this Earth.

Speak, Brother!

I can't bring myself to see another African-American kid killed for no better reason than "He looked at me the wrong way" or for a few dollars in his or her pocket.

I can't tolerate the excuses that people have for murder and mayhem, especially within the African-American community. Urban survival syndrome, the socio-economics of the inner city or the years of abuse inflicted by "the white man" on African-Americans do not and will not justify this senseless killing.

We are the first ones to decry the Klan or white supremacists who hang or kill one of "us," yet we don't have the same anger and passion when an African-American child lies in a pool of blood on a street – any street in this country – most of the time at the hands of another African-American.

Although we abhor the violence in Rwanda, Bosnia and Haiti, we Americans live in a war zone. Our kids grow up thinking that there are no consequences for their actions. When they commit a crime and go off to jail, only then do we begin to ask: "How did they go wrong?"

In barbershops, beauty salons, churches, board rooms, office buildings and editorial board meeting rooms, we continue to lambaste the "system" for not doing its job.

There is no "system." We are the "system."

The answers are not another jail, another prison or another set of laws.

The answer is for each American to make a complete commitment to treat one another with respect and decency, to share in restoring this country's soul.

Instead of calling a local elected official or some other "leader," I suggest we look in the mirror. That is where all problems – and answers – begin and end.

I suggest you turn off the television, put down that book and sit down and talk with your child. And don't forget to say, "I love you." But you must go beyond that.

You must also challenge yourself to reach as many children as possible and make them understand that their minds and an education will garner more respect than a gun.

I will cry for Reginald and Crystal. But I will also work to guarantee that before I take my last breath and write my last story, I will have done something to end the destruction of our society.

If each of us commits to the restoration of the hearts and souls of our respective homes and communities, we will leave our children in a safe place.

The question is not "What went wrong?" but "What am *I* going to do?"

In search of Jesse Jackson

July 11, 2001

NEW ORLEANS – As he made his way through the crowds, the famous man in the gray sports coat went through a routine that he has done countless times at these kinds of gatherings.

He hugged and kissed old friends, pulled others aside for private chats, and gave an interview or two for an awaiting journalist.

His body language was saying, "business as usual," but the eyes of the Rev. Jesse Jackson Sr. told a different story.

They darted across the dark spaces behind the main stage at the 2001 NAACP convention, seemingly searching for something – someone – that was lost, misplaced or misguided.

His usually beaming smile seemed to be forced. Gone was the ebullient personality that lit up rooms and made even political enemies subject to laugh with him.

His face appeared to be tired and haggard. The always-traveling Jackson has battled fatigue and exhaustion for a number of years, but this tired look was different. It seemed as if something was eating at him on the inside, which as we all know is clearly projected externally. I didn't ask and he didn't tell, but watching him for that brief period spoke volumes to my spirit.

Sure, he is still greeted as "The Reverend." Yes, the throng of youth at the ACT-SO competition Sunday leapt to their feet and cheered loudly when he strode onto the stage and launched into his all too famous "I Am Somebody" mantra. But it wasn't delivered with the same vigor. And when he was introduced prior to Julian Bond's speech Sunday night, the applause was nice and polite. That never happened to Jesse in the past, especially in front of an audience that adores him. Even when NAACP President Kweisi Mfume thanked him publicly, raising his voice to say how much Jesse was appreciated, the crowd didn't go along him. It was as if the preacher was hooping and the rest of us waited until he moved on to his next point.

My point? The Jesse we know; the Jesse we love; the Jesse we cherish; and yes, the Jesse we sometimes despise, is missing. But unlike other missing case reports, Jesse Jackson Sr. is not gone. There is no need to dial 911.

He is here in body, but the spirit that once seemed to revolve around him has vanished. And many are wondering when it will return.

When news broke in January that Jackson was the father of a young baby girl borne out of an affair with the former head of his Rainbow/PUSH D.C. office, a lot of people were stunned. Others immediately came to his defense, quoting the Bible and saying that a man without sin can only cast stones. A few called the news an effort by the GOP and others to silence the voice of a freedom fighter.

33

Speak, Brother!

Jesse himself promised to take some time off, spend it with his wife and family, and get himself together before continuing his civil rights and labor efforts.

That lasted three days, and he was soon back on the road.

Yet he has not been the same Jesse Jackson. He seems to be wandering aimlessly from one place to another, trying to find his way and reclaim the spot on the collective black mantle that made him the most recognizable black figure in the nation. He is clearly embarrassed and ashamed of what has taken not place. Not just the fact that his private indiscretions are now public, but that his reputation has been tarnished.

Maybe the Jesse Jackson we all know and have gotten used to will return – although it will never be the same - when he makes a real effort to apologize and seek forgiveness for his actions.

I'm not one to suggest that I am perfect and without sin. I also readily accept that in a man of God, the "man" always comes before "God." But an effort to simply push aside the devastating news of a child and a long-time affair is not as simple as Jackson and his staunch supporters have tried to make it.

This man preached to young men and women about teen pregnancy and morals and values. He counseled President Clinton through his affair with Monica Lewinsky; railed against Republicans for their moral absence in dealing with the poor; and he offered hope to the hopeless. He chose and accepted a position that is higher than others. And with that comes responsibilities.

The bottom line: he let his family down, and more importantly, he let himself down.

But Jesse is in denial. He wants and expects us to simply accept his partial and flimsy apology, issued immediately after the story broke, and move on as if it were the good ol' days. He doesn't want to address the issue at its core. In essence, he wants us to act as if it never happened. But it's not that simple. Everything that he has touched is coming under fire, ranging from his personal finances to those of the organizations he heads.

As a result, he has been rendered impotent in his attempts to serve as the champion of causes for those who can't speak up for themselves. The only person to blame for this is the man in the mirror.

And I guess that is the greatest loss in all of this. At a time when the helpless need a champion, the former lieutenant of Dr. Martin Luther King Jr. is off the field, nursing a concussion, while trying to get back in the game.

But the game never stops. It only keeps going with new players. Even if they aren't as good and talented as the first team, the game still must be played. And the Rev. Al Sharpton and others, despite their denials, are making a move to become "the man."

Jesse, if you are reading this, do something your good friend Ted Kennedy successfully accomplished. A few years ago when he was close to losing his

Speak, Brother!

Senate seat, Teddy went to the JFK School of Government at Harvard University, made a public act of contrition and apologized for all of his misdeeds, and promised to return as the fighting liberal of old.

The result? He went out, kicked his opponent's butt and went on to regain the respect that he lost.

Maybe it's time for Jesse to do the same. It's time for him to truly look himself in the mirror and say, "I screwed up and let so many people down. Let me face my critics, truly apologize for my actions, and regain the public's trust." Privately, take some time to really renew your family relationship. And then take a personal sabbatical just for yourself. And then release it. Let it go.

Publicly, go back to your old school, North Carolina A&T, bring your family, friends and allies. But keep them seated on the front. At this time, on this day, you must stand at the podium – alone – with all eyes on you.

If that news conference takes three hours, so be it. But a written statement and a hastily called press gathering will not suffice. It must be planned, orderly and packed with substance. I am in no way trying to exact my pound of flesh. We must not only hear, but also believe, that you are truly sorry. Release it; let it go.

Until then, the Jesse of old will forever be lost. He'll still get applauses, but they won't be thunderous. He will seek to speak out on truly important issues, but his voice will just be another voice. Not only will that be painful to the man himself, who has accomplished so much with so little, but also to the countless others who could benefit from his presence.

Boycotts are necessary to force change

April 4, 2002

About the only thing that has gotten some white Americans to fully understand and respect black America has been through the withholding of that green colored paper.

Lest anyone believe that the moral issue led officials in Montgomery to cave in to the year-long boycott of the bus system in 1956, it was the thought of losing millions of dollars once they realized that black folks were going to keep on walking and sharing rides in order to end segregation on buses. Many department stores and restaurants changed their "whites only" policy because they didn't want to see their business dry up as fast as a puddle in Houston in August.

Were it not for blacks pressing America to endorse an economic boycott of South Africa's racist and deadly apartheid government, Nelson Mandela would still be in prison.

South Carolinians are still angry at the tourist dollars that have stopped coming into the state because of NAACP protests of the Confederate flag. Even the threat of a boycott has sent some white folks scurrying like mad to make amends (remember the quick Texaco settlement that resulted in $187 million for black employees?).

That same tactic is being used in Cincinnati as some black activists have steadfastly endorsed a plan to keep celebrities and conventions out of the city until police and elected officials make amends for the racially-charged climate that led to riots last year. A number of city leaders, some of them black, have blasted the boycott as unproductive and racially divisive. Their comments are understandable considering they want those tourism dollars to continue to flow into city coffers.

But when some folks have protested, led marches, written letters and demanded accountability for the continuing problem of black men being shot and killed by police officers, then an economic boycott is what's needed to get some to face reality and deal with the problem.

When all else fails, African Americans and others have no other choice but to hit the pocketbook in order to cause changes to be made. But this is not solely a U.S. tactic. In Zimbabwe, a labor slowdown was ordered to protest the recent elections. Such measures have also been taken in other countries.

The favorers of the status quo always lament boycotts and protests because they hate negative publicity and want to change things "in due time." If that attitude was allowed to prevail, I wouldn't today be able to drink out of the courthouse water fountain!

What's even more appalling is when they use the tactic by saying that some black businesses will be hurt by the boycott efforts. Yea, so what's your point? There will always be pain when efforts are made for everlasting change. Some argued that black porters would lose their jobs when A. Philip Randolph organized the Brotherhood of Sleeping Car Porters. They did. There were black ministers who told Martin Luther King Jr. to shut up because their good thing was being unsettled by his call for and end to segregation. An effort has always been made to pit blacks against other blacks to keep things just as they are. That's called acquiescence; substantive work – hard work – is required if we don't want our kids and their kids to suffer the horrors of today.

Advocates of change in Cincinnati have the right to ask Wynton Marsalis, Whoopi Goldberg, Bill Cosby and others to stay home and not come to the city. Cincinnati city leaders can't continue to ask black folks in that town, which was named one of America's most segregated cities, to allow them time to get their act together. A mass movement to root out segregation should have taken place after the first death, but 15 deaths since 1995?

The Cincinnati boycott, as well as those in South Carolina and others cities, should continue as long as the leaders can continue to push it. Didn't the forefathers of America use the same strategy to protest with a little tea in the Boston Harbor?

If their actions of civil disobedience led to the formation of the United States, then maybe we should hope for the same monumental change in Cincinnati.

NAACP outdated? Think again

July 24, 2001

As the NAACP's recent convention reached a conclusion, I was instant messaging a friend from California who asked, "What in the hell is the NAACP doing now?!"

She was responding to an e-mail I sent her regarding the Adam's Mark boycott, the lawsuit against the paint industry over lead paint, the vote to condemn the Mississippi Confederate flag, and a number of other issues taken up at the group's annual confab.

This sister, like so many other folks I've talked with lately, was of the mindset that the organization had lost its way and was getting further and further away from its mission as the chief defender of civil rights for African Americans.

They contend that lawsuits against the paint industry, despite the fact that more African American children suffer from lead paint poisoning than any other, is unnecessary.

But the only thing that was furthest from the truth was the misguided belief that the NAACP was moving beyond its boundaries and into unchartered territory.

For most of its 92 years the prevailing focus of the organization was ending segregation and fighting for integration. Everything from securing voting rights to fighting for black students to enroll in college to outlining legislation was paramount to the NAACP.

But the fight today no longer is as easy as it used to be. Today's bigot doesn't stand on a street corner with a bullhorn shouting, "No Negroes allowed." They don't crack you over the head with a pipe for trying to order a hamburger. Nor do they stand in the door to prevent you from entering college.

Instead, today's challenge to hate and bigotry is waged against a stealth-like enemy. The fights are against judicial nominees who espouse a strict constructionist view of the Constitution, which is only double speak for keeping it for the chosen few. They are waged against corporate titans like Texaco and Coca-Cola, who make the effort to hire African Americans but place institutional barriers to prevent them from advancing upward. And they are against industries that continue to dump hazardous materials in minority neighborhoods, yet plead ignorant to higher instances of cancer, brain tumors and other maladies as a result of their activities.

A new day requires new tactics, new leadership, and a new way of thinking.

What other civil rights organization is carrying the ball today in advancing the agenda of election reform after the debacle in the recent presidential campaign? What organization is tackling, on a whole scale, the whitewashing

39

Speak, Brother!

of television and movies? What organization continues to answer thousands of calls a day regarding police harassment and racial profiling? What other organization has taken on the task of fighting for a national hate crimes law?

Let it be clear that anyone who merely suggests that the NAACP is an organization that is adrift is someone ignorant to the issues that face African Americans each and every day. But the National Association for the Advancement of Colored People also no longer focuses on those who are just of African descent.

As one high-ranking NAACP official put it, "Colored comes in all colors."

NAACP President Kweisi Mfume and board chairman Julian Bond, recognizing the changing demographics of communities across the country, have made overtures to reach out to Latinos in the effort for equality.

While some Hispanic leaders want the NAACP to take a back seat because of their increasing numbers, let's not fool ourselves. Latinos have yet to reach the level of influence and regard as the NAACP. How can I make such a statement? The National Council of La Raza held its national convention last week in Milwaukee and the only news to come out of that gathering was when Mfume showed up. And when was the last time you saw the League of United Latin American Citizens take a forceful stand against issues of hate and bigotry?

It is truly amazing to see how so many people – and I counted myself among this group at one time, despite being a founding member of the NAACP at Texas A&M University – who have taken the view that the NAACP means nothing and has no bearing on their lives.

It is painful to hear African Americans who hold prestigious and high-paying jobs make such dismissive comments about the organization that fought the battles for them to land their jobs.

Take for instance the diatribe of the Rev. Jesse Lee Patterson, the founder and president of the Brotherhood Organization of a New Destiny, and a member of the conservative group, Project 21.

In a recent column, Patterson praised the NAACP's past accomplishments, but went on to say it has "sold out the original intent of the organization," and called it a "tool of the elite, socialist wing of the Democratic Party."

Patterson, who is not alone in his thoughts, rhetorically asked, "What is the NAACP doing about the real problems in the black community? What is it doing about our schools, where our kids know more about condoms than mathematics? What is the NAACP doing about the 70 percent of black babies born out of wedlock? The NAACP has health and education programming, but the group's leaders spend more time in the media spotlight focusing on the trivial rather than addressing the true needs of black America."

I could go on, but you can easily gather what direction Rev. Patterson is headed in.

Speak, Brother!

It is downright silly of Patterson and others to make the comment, "What is the NAACP doing about the real problems of black America?"

The fact of the matter is the organization is doing just that. But there is no one organization that can do it all. And think about it: name one black organization that, despite all of its past successes and troubles, has the power to do what the NAACP continues to do? I don't see Rev. Patterson's organization, which I've never heard of, assume a leadership role on a wide scale and take the place of the NAACP.

No, it is not an organization that is without issues. But I can't sit here and complain about what it's not doing without asking Rev. Patterson and his fellow critics, "What are you doing?"

I am not of the belief that the NAACP is the be-all-to-end-all. Even Mfume, when speaking of the organization's study of the television industry, noted that the organization can't do it all.

But despite what you may think or hear, I have seen what the organization is capable of, and refuse to join the chorus of ignorant people who cannot offer support and praise for what the group continues to do.

The NAACP does not need any further detractors. What it needs are individuals who can bring vitality and vigor to advance the black agenda into the next century. I will forever hold the organization accountable, not only as a journalist but as a member (Yes, I've put my money where my mouth is and re-upped my membership).

Rev. Patterson, you are right in that we have some serious problems in black America. But calling for a boycott of the NAACP only makes our lives worse. I think it is ultimately silly to sideline the one organization that has been on the frontline for all of these years.

Walking in the spirit of those who came before us

Jan. 22, 2002

As the 40 mostly black faces walked silently down the North Court Street sidewalk in Athens, Ohio, yesterday, many faces peered out the windows of restaurants and quaint shops wondering what the gathering was all about.

Although school was out at Ohio University because of the Martin Luther King Jr. national holiday, many students took the day off to hang out, grab a bite to eat with friends or catch a movie. Their movement was no different than what you would find in any college town. But on this day, they got a chance to see something that happens only in symbolic gestures: African Americans walking down the street in an effort to rekindle the glory days of the Civil Rights Movement and pay homage to the ancestors who went before us.

As the keynote speaker at the Alpha Phi Alpha Fraternity's Phi chapter MLK Day event, I joined the students, which included some white and Latino brothers and sisters. We walked from Baker Hall to the Mt. Zion Church where King spoke in 1959. And as we walked down the street, I couldn't help but look at all of the nearly all-white faces staring back at us.

Many of them were unsuspecting and they didn't expect to see us. They were laughing and talking, enjoying the day, as any reasonable person would expect. But as we approached each window you could see conversations stop and some turn around to see what was going on. As I looked at their eyes I wished I had the opportunity to listen in on their thoughts and read their minds. You could tell some were wondering what the walk was all about, even though the brother in the front of the crowd held in his hand a large color photo with the likeness of the Rev. Dr. Martin Luther King Jr.

I must admit that walking down that sidewalk wasn't as chilling to my soul as methodically walking down the quiet road in Jasper, Texas, where James Byrd Jr. was brutally dragged to his death four years ago. But a chill did go up my spine as I reflected on those white faces and how just 40 years ago what the reaction would have been.

We've seen the videos, read the stories and listened to the survivors recount the bloody days of civil unrest in cities across the country as African Americans decided that they were sick and tired of being relegated to second-class citizenship, and that whether they lived or died, Jim Crow was going to be buried once and for all.

We walked by each of the windows with a steady pace, and as a result, I couldn't stop and look deep within the souls of each individual. Anyone who studies body language will tell you that you can learn a lot by studying someone's eyes. It seems that their entire character is given away just by

Speak, Brother!

peering into those eyes, going back to the back of their head and traveling down to the bottom of their soul. The eyes, indeed, say a lot.

And as I looked at their faces my mind kept going back to the faces and blood thirsty eyes of men and women in the 1950s and 1960s who, when they saw peaceful protesters, they would react with such hatred and anger, often played out with their fists and feet. Although our march was symbolic, it looked just like what we have seen on countless occasions.

I couldn't help but wonder, "Roland, if this was 1960 and you were walking down the streets of Alabama or Mississippi and one of those white thugs dropped their sandwich and came out swinging at you, what would you do?"

I shuddered to think that I would be willing to accept a beating at the hands of someone who I've never met and have never done anything to. Could I be as bold and challenging as a Martin Luther King Jr., Ralph Abernathy, Fred Shuttlesworth, Rosa Parks or the other countless and nameless souls who were willing to sacrifice their lives for a generation they would never see grow up? Watching the sea of white faces along North Court Street caused me to confront my innermost demons, as well as sing praises on high for what those before me had done.

I wished for a moment that I had a video camera and could capture through the lense of a camera what my own lenses were seeing. I can't adequately describe what I saw and felt because it was the first time that I had ever seen what it was like "back in the day." Again, the circumstances were vastly different, but in my mind, it was just as real as if Bull Connor was standing on the next block, waiting for us to turn the corner to unleash his dogs and fire hoses.

There comes a time when a generation can't experience what it "used to be like." Jews today can show pictures and tell stories, but a 20-year-old Jew today can't remotely understand the Holocaust because he doesn't have firsthand knowledge. A 30-year-old black lawyer can't fully comprehend a thing when Maya Angelou or Julian Bond talks about their grandfather being born a slave. We can hear it, but we can't feel it coursing through our bones.

The great thing, while at the same time being sad, is that this generation has truly never had to experience the pain of seeing a "whites only" sign or having to be told to go to the back of the window to get your food. We can't know what we've never experienced. It is great because we haven't had to endure the daily pain of such indignities, yet sad because some today discount what others had to battle over.

I supposed in a way I'm eternally grateful for the march because I can now be able to say I know a little something about what it feels like to be alone on an island with a sea of white faces staring at you – some with a blank stare, others with disdain and a few with deep compassion. I'm grateful because that image will never be lost on me, and each time I read and watch stories about

Speak, Brother!

the Movement, I can truly say: I may not have walked in your shoes, but I for sure have walked in your spirit.

Michael Jordan and Jesse Jackson Sr.: Two peas in a pod

Sept. 28, 2001

How fitting that the week Chicago's big J – Michael Jordan – announces he is returning to the NBA, the Windy City's other big J – the Rev. Jesse Jackson Sr. – makes a stunning declaration that he may go to Afghanistan with a peace delegation and negotiate directly with the Taliban.

Some may find it silly to compare Jordan's quest to shut up all the naysayers who doubt his ability to withstand the rigors of the NBA at the age of 38 with that of what Jesse may soon do. Yes, Jordan is only trying to play basketball and Jackson is walking into a minefield that could very well cost him his life. But the interesting parallel lies in the fact that while Jordan so desperately seeks to answer the challenge, not only of his mind but his physical spirit, the good Rev has the same inner desire to show America and the world that he is still a relevant political and humanitarian figure.

The Bush Administration has gone to great pains to not publicly criticize Jackson –he has talked with Secretary of State Colin Powell and National Security Adviser Condoleezza Rice – who both said he's not prohibited from going and that the decision rests with him. But they clearly know his involvement – even if it means gaining the release of two Americans and six other foreign relief workers – could muddy an already delicate situation.

As one could imagine, critics are already sniping at Jesse's heels by calling him a shameless self-promoter. He announced on Thursday that he received a telegram Wednesday from Mohammed Sohail Shaheen, a spokesman at the Taliban's embassy in Islamabad. Yet Mullah Abdul Salam Zaeef, the Taliban's ambassador to Pakistan, disputed that, saying Jackson reached out to them and that Taliban leader Mullah Mohammad Omar "has accepted his offer to mediate between the Taliban and America, and we will provide him our best possible facilities to visit Afghanistan," according to the Afghan Islamic Press, a private news agency close to the Taliban.

Jackson later modified his remarks, saying some Pakistani-Americans acted as go-betweens. "It doesn't matter who initiated this, but that both of us are interested in talking," he said.

Jackson is clearly going to have to give a straight answer as to whether or not he was sought out or if he did the seeking – credibility and honesty are always a plus, especially when you have already lost the trust of so many. But he also is going to have to identify what his mission is. Securing the release of the eight relief workers is a worthy effort; trying to arrange the surrender of Osama bin Laden falls outside of the scope. America must respond to the vicious attack on the World Trade Center and Pentagon and even the Rev can't stop that from happening.

Speak, Brother!

There is little doubt that the services of Jackson could be beneficial, especially to those families with loved ones who are being held. But it could also be a boon to Jackson's reputation, which has been significantly tarnished since he was exposed earlier this year for having an affair that resulted in a young child. Ever since he admitted to the affair and child, he has engaged in a number of activities to repair the damage to his name and reputation in order to maintain his legitimacy as a moral leader of America.

Despite the negative baggage that he has packed himself, we must be honest and admit that the man does have some experience in this area. He made a name for himself 15 years ago by leading a delegation of black ministers to Syria and securing the release of U.S. Navy Lt. Robert O. Goodman Jr., who spent a month in Syrian custody after his plane was shot down.

That same year he came home from Cuba with 48 Cuban and Cuban-American prisoners. In 1990, he was the first American to bring hostages out of Kuwait and Iraq, and in 1999 he secured the release of three American soldiers captured by Serbs in Yugoslavia.

Jackson says he doesn't want to go, but we all know that deep down, he would relish the opportunity to show President Bush, many of his former friends and supporters, and of course the Rev. Al Sharpton – who has been trying to elevate himself to Jackson's level – that he still has the Midas touch when it comes to coming home with hostages after others said he would fail.

Just as I don't doubt the resolve of Michael Jordan in showing everyone this year that he is the best man to ever lace 'em up, my money is on Jesse pulling off a miracle in Afghanistan.

May God be with you, Brother Jesse.

Million Man March one year later: Still no regrets

October 27, 1996

Every few months since this time last year, I've found myself thumbing through the stack of color photos that occupy a space in my home office.

I smile when viewing the photo of the African-American grandfather holding his grandson above his shoulders so he can squint his small brown eyes to see the figures gathered on the steps of the nation's capitol.

I can't help but laugh when remembering the boisterous shouts of 'Chicago! Dallas! Miami!' as brothers from across the country hugged, kissed and embraced one another as if they were long-lost members finally reuniting after years of separation.

And I guess in a sense the million-plus Black men who gathered in Washington, D.C., on October 16, 1995, were indeed long lost men, seeking a chance to rebuild the many lost years, and planning for a better future.

I attended the Million Man March as a part of my duties for KKDA-AM because our radio station broadcast it all across Dallas-Fort Worth on the day of the march. But even if I had not been working, there is no doubt I would have been a part of the sea of humanity that walked along the Mall on Washington, showing a tremendous amount of unity this nation has never seen.

There were many, namely some Christian preachers, who tried to discourage Black men from attending the march. They, as well as other critics, focused much of their attention on Louis Farrakhan's Islamic religion and Ben Chavis' past problems with the NAACP. But in many respects, their sounds of alarm were ignored by many because of a louder alarm – that of the Black man under attack.

The march was billed as a Day of Atonement for African-American men to atone for their past mistakes and to pledge to return home and rebuild their homes, churches, families and lives. Many said the mission and objective of the march was too vague and needed to be more focused on specific causes and concerns.

While I understand those who have said that march planners failed to capitalize on the tremendous energy created in Washington, D.C., I disagree with the notion that it was a failure.

There is no amount of money I could receive that could replace the sheer pleasure I received in seeing Black men who did not know each other hugging, kissing and pledging to be better men.

I grew up in an all-Black neighborhood and have spent the better part of my life surrounded by people who look like me, and it's not common to see Black men behaving in such a fashion.

Speak, Brother!

I can't overlook my feeling just before the march and after when I would see a Black man across the street, and instead of flashing a menacing look, we exchanged smiles.

My memories are quite vivid as I recall walking up the steps of the capitol at 5:30 in the morning, looking to set up for my live news reports. Failing to get to the right location due to a bit of disorganization, I had to cut across the crowd and climb over the wall. And what happens? Black men grab both of my arms, take my bags and lift me over the wall, shouting, "Hey, let the brother through! He's got to broadcast the march back to the people in Dallas!" Yes, my bags were still there. Yes, my wallet was still in place. And I can't help but recall one brother saying, "Just tell the people the truth and what really happened. Peace."

I don't know his name and couldn't even place his face. But it was such an act of kindness that reminds me of the self-worth and importance of the Black man and what this march meant for this country, but more importantly, for our race and as individuals.

We all know about the trials and tribulations faced by Black men: More of us in prison or a part of the criminal justice system; most likely the first to lose a job; underpaid; overworked; downtrodden and in many cases, forgotten.

But the march was in a sense the injection many of us needed to go forth and do the job our ancestors expected us to do.

The legacy of the Million Man March, unlike the 1963 March on Washington, will not be remembered for what the man at the podium said. It will be recalled for what Black men did at the march and after.

No, I can't offer you any hard figures to justify that the march was a quantified success. We'll never know if Black voter registration went up, crime went down or if more Black businesses were created as a result of the march.

But I can say that I have seen a change of attitude of many of my friends, be they Protestant, Muslim, Democrat, and Republican, young or old. I have personally witnessed a transformation in many brothers who were unforgiving and self-centered. Many of them are now more patient and willing to give more of themselves to help our people.

The march was not about speeches. It was about the Black man who returned home and after dating his woman for eight years, decided it was time to marry. It was about the Black man with four children from different mothers who vowed to begin paying child support, even if he had to get a second job. And it was about the people – not Farrakhan, Jesse Jackson, Chavis or any of the athletes and entertainers present – standing up with their heads in the air and backs upright.

This march was for us and for us only. It was about Black men reaffirming themselves and sending a statement to all of mankind that we can do for ourselves.

Speak, Brother!

It took me nearly all day last year trying to figure out what I would say when we ended our broadcast. And I remembered a quote James Baldwin made after the 1963 March on Washington that will no doubt, at least for me, sum up the impact of the 1995 Million Man March: *"That day, for a moment, it almost seemed that we stood on a height, and could see our inheritance; perhaps we could make the kingdom real, perhaps the beloved community would not forever remain that dream, one dreamed in agony."*

Juneteenth: My images are changed

June 19, 1994

As a child growing up in Houston, Juneteenth has always represented an opportunity for my five siblings and me to join our aunt and uncles and cousins for a day of food, fun and relaxation at the neighborhood park.

Dad and Mom would load up the rusty, gray barbecue pit on the back of a borrowed truck and remind my brother and me not to forget our baseball mitts, swimming trunks and the insect repellant.

It was nothing for our little picnic to expand into a gathering that could quickly rival any family reunion (My grandmother and grandfather had eight kids and nearly 50 grandkids. I stopped counting a long time ago).

Even though the holiday represented the freeing of slaves in Texas long before we were born, to us it was a time to run uninhibitedly throughout the sprawling park and eat until our little tummies were about to burst.

Yet as I have grown older, the holiday has meant more to me than a parade, party or family get-together.

It has meant a chance to reflect on the shock – and possible anguish – of learning that you were free 2 ½ years earlier than when Gen. Gordon Granger arrived on the shores of Galveston on June 19, 1865, to read the Emancipation Proclamation.

It must have seemed odd to know that while you were laboring under the hot sun and ever-present whip of a slave master, your fellow African brothers and sisters in South Carolina, Georgia and Mississippi had been reveling in freedom.

But instead of unleashing their anger at the messengers who delivered the late word, those African slaves grasped their freedom to make their homes and cities a better place for themselves and their children.

Juneteenth, for me, is no longer about the parade or concert at the park. It is a time to focus and celebrate on the impact that Africans and their descendants have had on the Lone Star State. Yet many of these true Texan heroes don't get the recognition of a Stephen F. Austin, Sam Houston or Mirabeau B. Lamar.

I think of Matthew Gaines, who, according to Texas A&M University history Professor Dale Baum, served as "the most forceful, charismatic and militant black leader in Texas politics during Reconstruction."

It was Gaines, and the 13-member black delegation of the 12th Legislature, who were instrumental in the establishment of the Agricultural and Mechanical College of Texas, now known as Texas A&M University.

My personal celebration recognizes my Alpha Phi Alpha Fraternity brother Heman Marion Sweatt, whose lawsuit against the University of Texas Law

53

Speak, Brother!

School in February 1946 forced the white-ruled institution to open its doors to African-Americans and other minorities.

The soul and hope of black Texas was furthered championed by Barbara Jordan, who, in the mid-'70s, became the first Southern woman to be elected to Congress since Reconstruction.

As her authoritative and articulate voice resonated through the House of Representatives, Jordan brought a presence, spirit and exuberance for the Constitution that rivaled anyone to ever grace Congress.

And who can forget Jack Johnson, the man raised on the beaches of Galveston who became the first black heavyweight champion of the world.

Countless African-American heroes have left their indelible impressions on the state of Texas.

So while African-Americans and other Texans fan out to eat a little potato salad, listen to some blues or jazz, or just curl up under a tree with a good book, take a little time to thank those African and African Americans who came before us and worked to allow us to celebrate our freedom.

SECTION TWO
ENTERTAINMENT

Halle and Denzel: Seeing prosperity through years of pain

March 28, 2002

When Halle Berry's name was called Sunday night as the winner in the Best Actress category at the Academy Awards, I tried with all my power to literally shake the foundation of my home with a booming yell.

Not only was I happy to see this talented and gorgeous sister rewarded for her work in *Monster's Ball* – the first time she has ever been nominated for the prestigious award – it was clearly a breakthrough for the years black women have toiled in relative obscurity in Tinsletown.

Critics at such media entities like Salon.com have criticized Halle for the tears she shed; some even called it a near-nervous breakdown. But no critic was as shameful, pathetic and cynical than Richard Corliss of *Time* Magazine, who managed to weave in remarks about her hit-and-run accident, past abusive relationships and being the product of an interracial marriage. That's a disgrace and should be noted as such.

Others have suggested, and they include a number of African Americans, that she should have been more dignified in her response and not allow the moment to overwhelm her.

These are the kinds of folks who turn off the lights and throw everyone out of the house to end a good party. It is easy to criticize Halle and all the fuss being made about her win and that of Denzel Washington's for Best Actor because they played negative roles. But people should show some respect for an individual's performance and the historical nature of the win.

Regardless of what any of us want to say or think, black female actresses have gotten the scraps in Hollywood. The industry has been far more accepting in providing strong roles for black men then they have for black women. As men, we often don't want to recognize all of the things that black women – and women in general – must face when getting acting roles. There is the constant slapping down of some men who want to put you in their movie if you go to bed with them. There are the demeaning roles of "the sex object," which have nothing to do with one's talents.

Use your imagination to recall the many rejection letters and doors slammed in the face of Halle and other women after a casting call. Think about the roles she had to take that required her sexy figure to be more prominent than her skills. Sit back and imagine spending thousands of dollars on acting lessons, and the best you could get in a film were a couple of lines.

Black women like Hattie McDaniel and Whoopi Goldberg have been honored with Best Supporting Actress Oscars. Yet we all know that the pinnacle of any actor's career is to be considered the leading man and the leading lady. Having your name above the marquee in Hollywood is the same as being the CEO of a company: you're the top dog. And when you have to

Speak, Brother!

spend so much time and energy fighting the battles of race and sexism, even the most dogged and determined woman can give up.

You don't have to be Halle Berry or an actor to understand all of this. Imagine yourself receiving an award for something you did. Didn't you think back on all that you had to go through to get to that moment and how it felt good to be validated for the hard work and perseverance? I've been there. And like Halle, I've cried my butt off.

Halle's tears also can be tied to the spirit of the woman she has carried around with her for so long: Dorothy Dandridge. There is little doubt that Berry crossed a serious threshold when she did *The Dorothy Dandridge Story* for HBO. She spent six years trying to get the movie made, and she clearly identified with the struggles of Dandridge and how they somewhat parallel her own.

Ever since doing the Dandridge movie, which won her an Emmy and other accolades, Berry has talked about having a newfound sense of history, purpose and courage to take on more demanding roles. Prior to it, she admitted to being a fragile ego that wasn't sure what her place was in the business.

And when you walk in the shadows of those who came before you, it's proper to recognize them when you do well. I, too, was in tears thinking of what Lena Horne, Dorothy Dandridge and in the words of Halle, what "every nameless, faceless woman of color" had to endure in order that a Halle Berry could stand on that stage one day.

Those tears are similar to those I have shed when remembering A. Philip Randolph and the Brotherhood of Sleeping Car Porters and the struggle they had to endure to be unionized. The tears have come when listening to a speech by the Rev. Dr. Martin Luther King Jr. as he discussed his faith in God while staring death in the eye. The tears flowed in 1984 when Jesse Jackson stood before an audience at the Democratic National Convention, giving a sense of pride and hope for another generation, much like the Fannie Lou Hamer's and Ralph Bunche's did for the previous generation. The tears I shed at the 1995 Million Man March weren't just for that day, but for the countless black men who were on the wall of the Vietnam War Memorial who didn't get a chance to come home.

My heart always aches and my soul forever hears the echoes of our ancestors when such accomplishments are made because my spirit tells me that when they were catching hell, they were saying, "I can't give up because someone will come along after I'm long gone to pick up the torch the continue the journey."

The day after Halle won the sun came up, people went to work, children were at school, the war continued in Afghanistan and peace was still a long way off in Israel. But we should be grateful that we got a chance to witness history.

Speak, Brother!

Hollywood may not suddenly open up the floodgates for black actors and actresses as a result of Halle and Denzel's big wins. But we can at least revel in knowing that the accomplishment of one sister as Best Actress in an overwhelmingly white Academy has been duly recognized. And maybe, like Halle said, there is a young woman out there who can turn to her mom or dad and say, "It can happen to me."

Black America, never allow our pain from days past to cause our souls to repress the praise of accomplishments present and future. Our ancestors didn't so why should we?

Cultural icons outside the mainstream

Sept. 4, 2001

There is a tradition here in the South that is commonly followed by African Americans. When a funeral procession is rolling down the street you pull over – whether they are on your side of the street or not – and allow the procession to continue unabated. In Louisiana, it is common for men in a car or standing on the street to remove their hats.

It has always been a pleasant sight to see such respect paid to the deceased, especially in a society that grows more callous and impatient each day.

Those images came to mind Friday when I read a rather insensitive and stupendous article by a *New York Post* writer, who lamented the stopping of traffic in New York to allow the horse-drawn carriage carrying the body of singer/actress Aaliyah to proceed from the funeral home to a nearby Catholic church.

Rod Dreher wrote that he felt such an honor should only be accorded for individuals such as presidents, royalty and people of influence.

"And Aaliyah? Most people – including, I would wager, 99 percent of those whose holiday-weekend travel will be delayed by her slow-moving equine hearse – first heard the singer's name in connection with her death," Dreher wrote.

"A public funerary gesture as dramatic as a horse-drawn cortege befits the dignity of very few people in anyone's lifetime. The family of Aaliyah, a beloved daughter but undistinguished singer of forgettable pop songs, does the poor woman's memory no favors with this tasteless gesture."

His comments drew a sharp rebuke from black New Yorkers; the Post had to increase security at its headquarters after receiving death threats. Also, activist Al Sharpton demanded action be taken against the writer, but New York Post editors stand by his column.

I agree with the position that Dreher has the right to say what he wants; that's a First Amendment right. But the greater issue centers around the ability to respect the deceased, the decisions of those left behind to honor their loved ones any way they choose to, and the continued arrogance and naiveté of white America towards those held in high esteem in non-white communities.

To suggest that Aaliyah was an "undistinguished singer of forgettable pop songs" is a clear example of someone admitting to their obvious ignorance.

Here was a young lady who "distinguished" herself by having a hit album by the time she was 15. Not only that, despite waiting five years between her second and third albums, her self-titled June release was highly sought after by the general public. Thirdly, she was a young woman who was ready to show her considerable skills in not one, not two but three motion pictures in

61

Speak, Brother!

the next two years. All of this, Mr. Dreher, by the age of 22. Now tell me how many people in this world have accomplished so much at such a young age?

But I have witnessed such nonsense before.

On March 31, 1995, I sat at my desk at the *Fort Worth Star-Telegram* and was perusing the news wires when I saw an emergency alert go across the wire: "Singer shot; held hostage."

Always one to jump at breaking news, I hurried to read the article and discovered it was about a young woman named Selena. "Who in the hell is that?" I asked myself.

As the minutes passed by and more alerts were posted, I continued to monitor the story. About an hour or two later, we were informed that Selena had died after being shot by the president of her fan club. Again, I had no clue who Selena was and really didn't think much about the impact of her death.

That is until I read a story that quoted a 9-year-old girl in San Antonio who said: "She was our Elvis."

I was stunned to see those four words, especially in light of how Americans – let's be honest, mostly white folks – have reacted since the death of Elvis on August 16, 1977.

I proceeded to walk into the office of Gary Hardee, the assistant managing editor at the time, to ask him if we were going to send anyone to Corpus Christi. He said, "I don't think so."

"Gary, I just read this article. I think we had better reconsider that," I told him. "It might make sense to ask the folks at *La Estrella* (our weekly Hispanic insert) to get their opinion."

After a bit of a debate, he still wasn't sure if we should do so. I then headed back to my desk and read two more bulletins noting that the *Houston Post* (since closed) and the *San Antonio Express-News* were planning on doing special sections, respectively, on her life.

Now folks, when a newspaper chooses to do a special section on someone's death, you can bet your weekly paycheck that that's a big deal.

The moment I saw that I ran back to Gary's office and said, "We've gotta do this." He still wasn't sure. Exasperated, I said: "Gary, if George Strait or Garth Brooks were shot and killed, we would dedicate the entire paper to them!"

After making a couple of calls to the folks at La Estrella, he agreed and we sent two reporters. Thank God! Only 70,000 folks showed up at a memorial for her, followed by huge memorials in Los Angeles, Houston, San Antonio and other cities around the country. *People* Magazine, not the most multicultural of magazines, dedicated a special commemorative edition to her, which sold tons of copies.

The moral of this story is simple: there are beloved figures in our society who live outside of the mainstream. I didn't know Selena, but to a huge segment of the public, she was bigger than Elvis. If you ask the average black

Speak, Brother!

person if they can identify the Grateful Dead or Phish, they would look at you like you were crazy. But the average white person would do the exact same thing if you asked them to point out Frankie Beverly and Maze.

Mr. Dreher and others like him – be they black, white, Hispanic, Native American or Asian – should always recognize that just because you don't know someone doesn't mean they weren't important or didn't have an effect on someone else's lives.

The same reaction has been had by non-followers of NASCAR who have been astounded at the yearlong reaction to the death of Dale Earnhardt, who has been called the Michael Jordan of auto racing. If you don't follow the sport, you just don't know.

You cannot dismiss the amazing reaction from individuals who have been touched directly or indirectly by Aaliyah. No one can estimate the worth of someone and whether he or she should be accorded a funeral for a princess.

Mr. Dreher, Aaliyah was a beloved, talented, beautiful and gorgeous queen who exhibited a level of maturity unmatched by others her age. She also defied the convention wisdom that to be a top singer in the hip-hop arena you must be foul-mouthed, wear outrageous clothes (or no clothes at all) and behave in a boorish way. She was exactly the opposite.

Instead of writing a piece that was headlined, 'Sure her death's tragic – but this is too much,' you should have been a journalist and instead asked, "What made this woman so special that she deserves this kind of send off?"

By asking the latter rather than stating the former, you would have heard a compelling and convincing story, and most certainly had a much better column.

Don't just thank God, represent Him

"Therefore, I urge you, brothers, in view of God's mercy, to offer your bodies as living sacrifices, holy and pleasing to God – this is your spiritual act of worship. Do not conform any longer to the pattern of this world, but be transformed by the renewing of your mind. Then you will be able to test and approve what God's will is – his good, pleasing and perfect will." Romans 12:1-2

There Sean "P. Diddy" or "Puff Daddy" or "Whatever-the-heck-we're-calling-him-this-week" Combs stood: wearing his trademark shades, a diamond-crusted cross resting on his bare chest (his shirt unbuttoned down to his navel), thanking God for being able to co-host the American Music Awards when a year earlier, he was in a courtroom on trial for weapons charges.

Combs should have been giving God all the glory. He got off and his former gal pal Jennifer Lopez wasn't tried. But his protégé, Shyne, got 10 years for shooting up a New York nightclub.

My issue isn't with Combs thanking God - I believe God should get continuous praise each and every single day. But wouldn't it be nice to see entertainers and celebrities not only continue to thank God, but represent him?

It is tiresome to hear Destiny's Child throw God's name all over the place, but put out a song called "Bootylicious."

"I don't think you ready for this jelly; I don't think you ready for this jelly; I don't think you ready for this; 'Cos my body too bootylicious for ya babe." Yea, right! Those are not the words young Christian ladies use to glorify God.

Mr. Combs was willing to thank God, yet a few months ago, he chose to be the centerpiece of a cover story in *Details* Magazine, surrounded by butt-naked women. I don't recall P. Diddy giving God the glory then.

Some would suggest that the critique of such shallow behavior is judgmental. I'm sure the e-mails will come flying in that my position is one rooted in jealousy or the attempt for one set of Christian values to prevail over another. It's not. The issue is simply this: God should not be pimped when we want to give him thanks for winning an award. Instead of yelling his name, we should make an effort to represent him in our walk. Like they say today, I'm just trying to keep it real.

Every single one of us is a sinner. There is no disputing that. But if we choose to walk in the way of the Lord, then we must carry ourselves as such.

If we want to represent ourselves as believers in the body of Christ, don't you think we ought to be extremely careful about all of the body we choose to flash to the general public?

Speak, Brother!

It is difficult for those in the entertainment industry to withstand the pressures to sing songs filled with sexual lyrics, produce videos that don't involve gyrating women or wear outrageous costumes that leave nothing to the imagination. But by not "conforming to this world" we should work to "transform" the world by saying, "No,

I'm not going to do it that way. If God has put me in this position to use my talents, I don't have to compromise who I am for the sake of a dollar."

What we desperately need today are men and women who are willing to not only stand up and praise his name, but also represent him in how they walk and talk.

On that same American Music Awards stage, Yolanda Adams won the award from Contemporary Gospel Artist of the year. Looking lovely as all get out, Adams didn't sacrifice her moral position by having to dress like Lil' Kim. Instead, she kept her integrity and allowed her light to shine through her body and clothes as opposed to having all of the lights on her (we don't even have to bring up the dress Toni Braxton, the daughter of a preacher, wore a few years ago to the Grammys). When she accepted her award, Adams didn't just thank God for the blessings, she spoke of the need to follow him and live in his will each and every single day.

I know her speech wasn't what many wanted to hear – heck, Snoop Dogg was sitting on the front row with Bishop Don "Magic" Juan, a pimp made famous by his role in *American Pimp* – but it was desperately needed in a place filled with hero-worshipping and decadence.

As a member of the media, I know first-hand of the power of words and images. That's why it would be wonderful to see someone like Combs or Destiny's Child use their enormous media access to match their actions with their rhetoric. Then let's see young brothers and sisters emulate that instead of the bling-bling lifestyle.

Let's celebrate 'us' for just a little bit

Oct. 10, 2001

A couple of months ago, Denzel Washington's new film, *Training Day*, was previewed at the National Association of Black Journalists convention in Orlando to much anticipation.

We were all told this was not the same Denzel. How true that was. He wasn't his usual lip-licking-smooth-talking-*People* Magazine-sexy self in this gripping film directed by Antonio Fuqua. In fact, his performance as a corrupt cop is riveting, stunning and simply Oscar material.

But just as the lights came up and Fuqua strolled onto the stage to answer a few questions, a number of brothers and sisters launched into a tizzy as they threw a flurry of questions and statements at the director. "Negative portrayal of black men." "Why did the white boy have to save the day?" "There are a lot of good black cops out there." "Why must a black man make a negative film about black people? We get enough of that from white folks."

The Q-and-A session wasn't being moderated, and I could tell it was about to get real funky. So when they brought out an additional mike, I grabbed it and began to play host because I sensed that Fuqua was about to end up as the main course at a dinner in which he thought he was a guest.

Fuqua amiably tried to answer their questions as politely as he could, but the jabbering only got louder. Sensing this was not the scene they conjured up, the movie's publicists decided to cut the session short and whisked him out of there as soon as possible. All I could do was shake my head at the nonsense. Several folks kept reiterating, "This was only a movie," but others didn't want to hear any of that. They simply wanted to argue the point about Training Day's violent nature and the use of a black cop as the corrupt one.

I felt their pain, but refused to accept it. It seems as if black folks can get far too touchy about some stuff, which often causes the real issues to go unnoticed. Much of this uneasiness stems from years and years of pain and suffering heaped upon us in a spiritual, physical, mental and emotional sense.

Yet it seems that instead of glorifying the ability to sustain ourselves despite that pain, we seem to wallow in a sea of despair that only keeps us in a state of perpetual agony.

Hollywood clearly has an abysmal record when it comes to telling the story of black folk. There is no argument there. But we seem to be putting black directors and actors through an unnecessary cleansing process. If they do a comedy film or sitcom we criticize them for telling jokes when there are so many other important subjects to discuss. If they do a serious film, we lament that it wasn't positive enough.

The same could be said of the criticism by black folks in other areas. During a recent profile on ESPN, Charles Barkley said some African Americans have

Speak, Brother!

blasted him for not giving more to charity, despite more than $3 million in donations he has made since entering the NBA.

The Rev. Jesse Jackson Sr. gets blasted all of the time by black folks – including the Rev. Al Sharpton and his aides – for not doing enough, but those same people don't seem to want to acknowledge that his good far outweighs the bad.

This month, BET's Robert Johnson adorns the cover of *Forbes* Magazine as it profiles the 400 richest Americans. Let me say that again: a black man is on the cover of one of America's prime magazines of capitalism to talk about how he became the first black billionaire.

Unfortunately, the article also details the complaints others have about Johnson and BET, namely that it has focused on videos and other lowbrow stuff, rather than telling the positive stories of African Americans. A lot of that stems from BET being the only major black cable network.

Such complaints aren't unwarranted. I, too, have issues and have had them with BET. But while I may criticize, I can also freely congratulate and thank Johnson for the positives of the network over the last 20 years. If you haven't been happy with BET, fine. But at least accept the fact that BET is the only major black-owned property that has been purchased above and beyond its real value. If you don't think so, reflect on the Berry Gordy's sale 13 years ago of Motown to MCA for $61 million. Five years later, it was sold to Polygram for $325 million.

And maybe that's where the issue really hits home for me. There is nothing wrong with criticizing, but at least speak words of affirmation and the positive contributions at the same time. Don't just criticize one film   because you think it could have been done differently. If so, go and make your own! Despite the amount of money he has made, Bob Johnson should be commended for the job he has done at BET, which includes building an institution that has created more black millionaires than any other black-owned company. I also don't see many other folks sticking it out there for 20 years and trying to build a black cable network.

Constructive criticism should be made to toughen all of us up and improve our institutions, not tear down. We have enough haters in doing our jobs without adding more to the mix.

25 years later, 'Roots' still in search of respect

Jan. 18, 2002

There is no event in the history of television that has arguably had the impact on our collective conscious than the airing of Alex Haley's *Roots* in 1977.

The assassination of Lee Harvey Oswald and the first landing on the moon are two historic televised events that could be considered more important. But when you think of all the television min-series, movies and sitcoms that have made us laugh or cry over the years, nothing has come close to what Roots did for the soul of America.

Just one decade after the tumultuous Civil Rights Movement and the rapid rise and subsequent fall of the black militant era, America was transformed and enlightened by the epic tale of a black man's quest to discover his past.

During the airing of the series, nothing moved – malls were empty, Las Vegas showrooms were virtually silent and families gathered around televisions to see Kunta Kinte, Kizzie and the other ancestors of Alex Haley. Can you imagine restaurants closing early because no one would eat past 7 p.m. because of a television show?

It was even more amazing that 130 million people would choose to watch a television show that exposed the one aspect of American history that we are so adept at avoiding at all costs – slavery.

The end result? Many people – white, black and Hispanic – chose to investigate their past, searching for long lost relatives and rediscovering who they are and where they came from. It also established ABC as a network that was focused on quality programming, especially at a time when it was the home of banal shows like *Love Boat, Happy Days, Laverne & Shirley* and *Fantasy Island.* Maybe that's why it's so galling that ABC, the network that originally chose to air the miniseries, opted to pass on a showing of the 25th anniversary.

ABC executives made the conclusion that they didn't think *Roots* could garner a large enough audience to merit a showing and that the concept pitched was uncreative. That's funny. ABC is the fourth out of the Big 4 networks and is responsible for giving us plenty of lame sitcoms that were cancelled after only a few weeks. But somehow *Roots* wasn't good enough for their primetime schedule. If they thought it was so uncreative, why not make some suggestions to beef it up?

In an age where there are so few quality shows featuring African Americans, ABC's decision is beyond comprehension. And it's even more hilarious that NBC has chosen to broadcast the anniversary special tonight. (The network used to be called the National Black Channel because of *The Cosby Show* and *A Different World,* only to revert to the No Blacks Channel with the

Speak, Brother!

emergence of shows like *Cheers*, *Friends* and *Seinfeld*, which had and have virtually no black folks).

Some could say that the legacy of *Roots* is that is has had an everlasting impact on America. But when it comes to blacks in Hollywood, much stayed the same. Despite a cast that was nearly all black, many of these fine actors did not get an opportunity to display their acting skills beyond the miniseries. I guess America didn't change that much.

But despite all of that, *Roots* stands as a series that has withstood the test of time. Many young African Americans and I suppose, all Americans, cannot relate to how so many of us felt when watching the original airing. Maybe that's why all of us should take the time to instruct those who didn't watch the original. We could also watch tonight's anniversary, and visit The Hallmark Channel, which will air the miniseries in its entirety beginning on Sunday night, or buy the VHS or DVD collection.

But for now, let's all prove ABC wrong and watch the NBC *Roots* anniversary special in large numbers. It would be wonderful for the programming folks at ABC to see NBC win the ratings war for Friday with a blockbuster hit. That would be fitting for their ridiculous decision.

SECTION THREE
POLITICS

SECTION THREE
FIGURES

Dems finally show some fight

March 18, 2002

The rejection of Charles Pickering by the Democrat-led Senate Judiciary Committee last week brought to mind that famous scene from *The Color Purple* when Adolph Caesar, looking at Oprah Winfrey's character when she began to laugh at the dinner table, said: "Oh, my God. The dead has arisen."

Congressional Democrats have consistently played nice with their Republican counterparts. Sure, there have been a few skirmishes here and there, but for the most part, they have tried to give their mates across the aisle a fair shot at judicial nominees and legislative action.

But the GOP has not been as fair when it comes to politics. Their attitude, which I must admit is admirable in an Art of War kind of way, is simple: "We seek to chart the course for this generation and the next, and niceties be damned."

During the Clinton Administration the GOP used every means to exact revenge on the president and his supporters, zealously using congressional committees and special counsels to investigate anything. A few months ago on NBC's Meet the Press, Vice President Dick Cheney conceded his party may have gone a bit too far in their efforts. Where was this viewpoint while the madness was taking place?

Republicans wanted a fair vote on the Pickering nomination, but let's go back a few years when Clinton nominated Dr. Henry Foster for surgeon general. The GOP didn't want to vote on his nomination, so they took a vote on whether they should take a vote. The answer was no and he was never confirmed.

President Ronald Reagan, followed by President George Bush and later Speaker of the House Newt Gingrich, ushered in this new wave of Republicanism by tossing out the gentlemanly actions of Congress and focused on ramrodding through a GOP agenda. And their fingerprints were also left on the judicial branch, where 12 years of Reagan-Bush, now followed by four, and possibly eight years of Bush II, will mean a judiciary that is outrageously more conservative than generations past.

While Democrats were asleep at the wheel, Republicans figured out that if you want to really leave a stamp on America, all you have to do is appoint young, aggressive and conservative judges to the federal bench; knowing full well that their interpretation of the laws of this country will always be the final word, all the way up to the Supreme Court, for the next 30 years.

That's why the Pickering nomination was so crucial for Democrats to let it be known to President Bush and his followers: if you expect to pack the federal bench with more arch-conservative judges, think again.

Speak, Brother!

Democrats had their chance during the eight years of Bill Clinton, but under the leadership of Sen. Orrin Hatch, the Republicans forced the president to abandon many of his nominees for "safe" choices. In essence, Hatch said that the federal bench didn't need more liberals. Of course, Democrats cried foul, but they never made the GOP pay for their sins. Instead, people like Missouri's Ronnie White didn't get confirmed (Attorney General John Ashcroft, then a senator from Missouri, fought his nomination), and attorneys like Eric Moye and Sheryl Wattley of Texas waited years before they finally gave up (Unlike Pickering, they never even got a chance at a hearing).

That's why it is so galling to see Sen. Trent Lott and the conservative bunch up in arms over the defeat of Pickering, a Mississippi judge whose conservative credentials were torn asunder by national women and civil rights organizations.

Pickering's supporters tried to bring out the blacks in Mississippi who supported the judge, but their personal views of him were overshadowed by those who didn't want a man of his temperament on the federal bench. In essence, they said what's good for Mississippi ain't necessarily what's good for the nation.

The Dems made it clear they didn't want a conservative jurist on the bench and the GOP doesn't like it. Is this any different than the "liberal" judges the GOP opposed? Sorry, ladies and gents. What's good for the goose is good for the gander.

The greatest outcome of the Pickering nomination fight is that Democrats have finally gotten around to standing up to the GOP and flexing their muscle. Lott and others are promising retribution, and that's fine. But the Democrats should assume the posture that if you take out one of mine, I'll take out three of yours.

Is this fair? No. Is this a sign of bipartisanship that the president promised when he came into office? No. Did you for a second believe the president when he said he wanted to bring the sides together? Not a chance. It all sounds good on the campaign trail and in commercials, but it's not realistic.

Politics is not a game for the meek. And despite the grandstanding you hear, it's not all's fair in love and war.

Democrats must finally shed their image of being soft and unafraid to fight. Senate Majority Leader Tom Daschle has finally gotten his troops to rally around one position and not be so far-flung in their desires. Sure, there are southern Democrats like Georgia Sen. Zell Miller who are nothing more than Republicans in Democrats clothing, but if Democrats expect to keep the federal judiciary fair and balanced, and position themselves for a real shot at the White House in 2004, they will have to toughen up.

Pickering's defeat is a good start.

Family comes first, even ahead of the President

April 24, 2002

As the news begin to spread about Karen Hughes resigning her post as advisor to the president for family reasons, the Washington press corps immediately began to ask the question, "What's the real reason behind her decision?"

It seems that many journalists and others inside of the Beltway – the rest of us call it Washington, D.C. – don't think anyone would leave such a powerful position unless they did something to tick off the president or was involved in an unlawful act. In the nation's capitol, power isn't given up so easily, especially when someone like Hughes is a close friend and advisor to the president.

But Hughes, considered to be the most influential woman to ever serve in the White House, says her departure is no mystery: family is her top priority.

"My son is going into the final three years of high school before he goes off to college, and we want him to have his roots in Texas as well," she said.

She later added: "This is a family-friendly White House, and I think this is a family-friendly decision. This says that I can do what is right for my family and continue to serve the president in a key way."

The decision by Hughes to return home to spend more time with her husband, son and friends could be seen as a sign that a woman can't handle the rigors of an intense job while maintaining a strong family. Over the years we as a society have forced women to make a decision between their careers or family. But an increasingly number of men and women are deciding that their jobs are great and pay well, but the quality of life issue is more important.

Ever since September 11, more and more people have concluded that living in a materialistic and power-hungry world where we are more concerned with climbing the ladder of success while leaving our husbands, wives, sons and daughters at home to live and grow without us is not for them. I can't even begin to explain the number of men and women who have no clue what goes on at home because they are so busy building a career.

I can recall one woman who remarked: "My job is me. It is who I am." My response was simple, "If you get fired, do you then die?"

This is not an issue that is limited to corporate executives. Many ministers spend more time flying around the country, speaking on family values, while their families eat dinner each night without him or her at the table. So many of us have packed workouts, facials, massages, dinner meetings and other "important" tasks into our schedules that we can't even remember the last time we had a romantic dinner with the spouse or played a board game with our children. The result of so much focus on job and money has left a generation of children with no concept of family time, and instead, a warped sense of what is important.

When children see mom and dad missing the important moments in life, it causes them to do the same when they become adults, and that's when a selfish pattern sets in that is destructive to the family unit.

It has always been my position that if there is a choice between making $50,000 and spending a lot of time with my wife and family, or making $300,000 that would require me to travel a lot, work long hours and not be able to play golf and the other things I enjoy, the $50,000 job would always be the choice. Yes, I have bills and would like to buy nice items, travel and do other things that money affords, but when my time on earth has passed and my children are raising their children, I would hope that the values of family over money would be instilled in them so that my legacy would extend from generation to generation.

If you are one of those workaholics who have always talked of wanting balance but never finding the time, take a moment and do a self-analysis to determine what is important in your life. If it's your job, fine. Yet don't keep saying family is important when you choose the career every time.

In choosing family over a job, you may have to accept less money, turn down a promotion or even walk away from a great job in order to find the happiness that you always desire. This will require you to possibly reduce your lifestyle, sell your house to move into another one that is smaller and more manageable, and make some other needed adjustments.

When you do, what you might find is that you are more refreshed and revived than you have ever been, and you will be able to enjoy those things in life that were once impossible to consider.

The spiritual significance of voting

April 10, 2002

As I watched car after car turn into the driveway of Good Lutheran Church yesterday, I couldn't help but get teary-eyed as I saw so many folks rushing in to stand in line to cast their votes.

There were men and women of all shapes and sizes, but most of the faces at this location had skin that was kissed by nature's sun. They stood patiently in line, some playing with their children, while others double-checked their voter registration cards to make sure they were in the right place. I eavesdropped on a few others who talked on cell phones, calling friends and loved ones to ask them if they voted, and if they said no, told them to hurry up because the polls would be closing soon.

A couple of women were heard remarking about having to stand in the line, which ran 30 deep at one point. But as the woman standing behind me said, "I'll wait. This is important."

My soul was happy to hear her comment and to see so many not care whether they had somewhere else to go or if dinner was ready; all they wanted to do was to get in that voting booth and mark their paper, scan it into the machine and go home knowing they did their part in participating in the American political system.

The emotions that rang in my spirit were largely due in part to recently returning from Birmingham and visiting the Civil Rights Museum, a stunning and magnificent structure that tells the story of the black struggle for equality.

Seeing the brutal photo images of black men dangling from trees; the white silk Klansman's robe behind a glass case; a replica of a bus with "colored section" signs adorning the back of the seat; as well as the stirring "I Have a Dream" speech by Dr. Martin Luther King Jr. made me sad, morose and weakened.

I could barely stand at times as I thought about so many who died and lived in agony during such wretched times. So many long for the days of old when Ozzie and Harriet were the model couple, but for many of us those days aren't filled with wonderful memories, but instead, a reminder of just how much America hated the black man and woman.

The pain and agony that permeated my bones continued as I watched and read about so many brothers and sisters vying for a right to vote, determined not to allow Jim Crow and his many protectors from stopping them from realizing that American dream.

I guess that's why I get so emotional when it comes to the simple act of voting. I never jump out of my car, rush in, grab the ballot, hurry up and pencil something in and dash out to the car so I can run some errands. I often take my sweet time, taking all of it in because when I do, the spirits of the

Speak, Brother!

ancestors are stirring in me. Can't you visualize that elderly brother in overalls at the table, painstakingly signing his name on the election rolls? You mean to tell me you don't see the beaming pastor with the black-rimmed glasses smiling with joy as he is handed a ballot and ushered into the voting cubicle? I suppose if not, you can't imagine the happiness of the brother on the street, giving you a thumbs up and thanking you for voting for him as he runs for the city council.

I see all of this when I go and vote. I think of the men and women who recently stood in line in Zimbabwe for two days, only to have Mugabe essentially steal the election. I can't get the images of the same taking place in South Africa – what seems like is years ago – to cast their ballot for Nelson Mandela.

Voting is such a spiritual thing for me because it is not a simple act but more of a continuation of what so many before me fought long and hard for. It's not so easy to dismiss as an act that won't mean much.

Even if the candidate I voted for loses the race, it doesn't matter. It's just the thought of knowing that I simply cast a ballot for an ancestor who died hoping they could one day.

Arafat must stop speaking out of both sides of mouth

March 30, 2002

As Israeli tanks rolled into the West Bank town of Ramallah, PLO leader Yasser Arafat frantically telephoned world leaders, hoping they could impress upon Israeli Prime Minister Ariel Sharon to stop the attack.

Respecting him as the recognized leader of the Palestinian people, they responded in the affirmative, only to be rebuffed by Sharon.

If only Arafat would have been so emphatic in demanding that Palestinian terrorists cease and desist their suicide bombings.

It seems that every time Arafat is pushed into a corner due to Israeli military action, he calls for a cease-fire and a renewed quest for peace.

In an interview with Reuters television, he appealed in English to the international community "to stop this aggression against our people, this military escalation, this killing."

Then, in Arabic, he added: "Together we will march until one of our children raises the Palestinian flag over the churches and mosques of Jerusalem," accusing Israel of "terrorist racist actions using all kinds of American weapons."

But why can't he do something before suicide bombers kill Israelis? It's easy to give an impassioned call for peace when you know Israel is going to strike with military precision in response to Jewish blood being shed. And after 30 Israelis were killed over a three-day period, Arafat and the world knew the Israeli government would not sit idly by. Also, Arafat will decry the suicide bombing in English, but he won't do so in Arabic, which is the language the bombers use.

The many factions of Arafat's Fatah movement all operate under his command, yet they continue to send suicide bombers in their quest for Palestinian statehood. That means two things: Either he has no control over the Palestinian militants and they have absolutely no respect for him or he is tacitly giving approval for the bombings.

By virtue of his refusing to absolutely and positively demand an end to the Palestinian violence, Arafat is determining his own fate, which will only lead to more deaths of Israelis and Palestinians and prevent peace from coming to the Middle East.

The Palestinian people deserve to live in their own country and not under the thumb of the Israeli government. But killing Israelis cannot achieve statehood. If Arafat and the PLO want peace, then killing is not the answer.

Arafat knows that, but he is also playing a major public relations campaign. He pleads ignorant to stopping the violence from his end while at the same time saying he is the recognized leader.

Speak, Brother!

That's the same as President Bush declaring he is the commander-in-chief of the United States military, yet playing dumb to knowing why U.S. armed forces are behind killings in other countries.

The same PR ploy was taken this week as Arafat played the role of victim when Israel refused to allow him to attend the Arab Summit. Then after 22 Israelis were killed in a suicide bombing, the summit gets behind a Saudi peace plan, which then puts world pressure on Israel to accept the plan. But we all knew Israel would respond, so now they look like bullies by pushing military action with a peace plan on the table.

Let's be clear: Israel is in no way absolved of their sins. The Israeli government has proved to be completely resistant to world demands in the past and Palestinian efforts to negotiate a peace plan, and have been to quick to declare military action.

But no one with common sense could expect Israel to watch their people die and not respond. President Bush acknowledged as much when he said Israel has a right to defend itself.

Both Israeli and the Palestinian people must stop their posturing before the world and truly commit to peace. Several of the PLO factions must toss away their attitude concerning a complete destruction of the state of Israel. That is no better than a refusal by Israel to back a Palestinian nation.

Yet none of this will be achieved as long as Arafat plays dumb and allow the terrorists under his watch to send suicide bombers into Israel. And all that does is take away his moral authority and make him an endorser of terrorism.

SECTION FOUR
9.11

SECTION FOUR

Mr. President, please, act like the President

Sept. 18, 2001

In the precious hours and days after the horrible tragedy in Washington, D.C. and New York, I must admit that it was a pleasant sight to see President George W. Bush put forth a strong and bold front.

The devastating attacks on the World Trade Center and the Pentagon were so horrendous that the only thing Americans seemed as if we could depend on was the strength from the commander-in-chief, who not only must be the face of America to the world, but he (and I hope one day she) must also act as the healer-in-chief.

Although nine months into his presidency, Bush's strong and measured words in the aftermath of seeking justice against the terrorists clearly showed that his view was consistent with that of what other Americans were saying.

"Make no mistake: The United States will hunt down and punish those responsible for these cowardly acts," he said hours after two planes crashed into the World Trade Center and another into the Pentagon on September 11.

Three days later at the National Prayer and Remembrance service, Bush issued a compassionate speech, as well as a matter-of-fact and chilling statement: "This conflict was begun on the timing and terms of others. It will end in a way and at an hour of our choosing."

But as the days progressed and the investigation began to result in arrests and more and more information about the hijackers, the language of the president began to take a turn for the worse.

September 15: "We're going to meet and deliberate and discuss – but there's no question about it, this act will not stand; we will find those who did it; we will smoke them out of their holes; we will get them running and we'll bring them to justice. We will not only deal with those who dare attack America, we will deal with those who harbor them and feed them and house them."

The feelings went from disturbed to appalling on September 17 as I witnessed a president, a native of my beloved Texas, lean back in his leather recliner and proudly say that he wanted terrorist Osama bin Laden, the Most Wanted Man in the World, "dead or alive."

"Did he just say what I think he said?" I asked myself. It only took a flick of the remote from CNN to FOX News for that question to be answered.

There is little doubt that a long and extensive war against bin Laden and terrorists in general will result in either his death or capture, but it still was crass and unsatisfactory for such a statement to roll off the tongue of the President of the United States.

It seems with each passing day the president's attitude reverts back to his trademark cocky and arrogant attitude that was evident at times during his presidential campaign.

83

Speak, Brother!

Despite precise, measured and forceful statements from Secretary of State Colin Powell and Vice President Dick Cheney, Bush seems to be taking on an air where he has to prove his manhood.

Some of the blame could be laid at the feet of his presidential advisers who have gone out of their way to show Bush is in full control of this national emergency. Presidential aides were reportedly working overtime to dispel the notion that the president was missing-in-action in the hours after the attacks when Air Force One couldn't immediately return to Washington, D.C. by portraying him as desperately wanting to return to the nation's capital.

But regardless of what his aides may be telling him, the buck stops with the president and he should be sticking to his initial comments without adding fuel to this already raging fire. Take a look at all of the radio and television talk shows and you will find your fill of tough talk from folks who are out for blood.

The United States of America is at war and the President of the United States is conjuring up thoughts of an old West poster stating, "Wanted dead or alive." Is this what we really need at this juncture?

Americans are clearly hurt, angry and highly ticked off at what has happened. Polls show more than 90 percent approve of the president's job during this crisis and 80-plus percent support attacking terrorists with military strikes. But this is an extremely sensitive and delicate situation.

No one knows if the terrorists have other attacks planned, and efforts are still being made to recover bodies at the crash sites. Also, America has to walk a tightrope in getting complete cooperation from the international community to track down and cut off the funding to bin Laden and his terrorist network. The last thing we need is a president who has taken on a smug attitude and acts like a cowboy running amok on the range.

Mr. President, you are the face of America. You are the one person who represents the attitudes that so many across the world are forming about the United States right now. We ask of you – no, we demand of you – to show strength, humility and focus in this time of crisis.

"Wanted dead or alive" is a cheap attempt at showing your manhood and exhibiting strength. You don't have to prove your manhood. You are, despite anger stemming from the presidential election, the President of the United States.

Act like it.

The whitewash continues

Oct. 4, 2001

Heeding President George W. Bush's call for America to return to normal, I am now ready to get back to doing just that. To my friends in the mainstream media: you continue to suck when it comes to diversity.

Yea, I know suck is such a strong word to use. But hey, I couldn't find any other word to express my anger and complete disdain at the lack of diversity of talking heads in the wake of the September 11 attacks on the World Trade Center and the Pentagon.

Heeding the call for unity and healing, I have tried in vain to stay away from writing about racial issues in the wake of this attack that has killed more than 6,000 Americans without regard to race, religion or sex. A brother has been patient. But after watching last night's *Nightline*, along with all of the cable channels and networks since September 11, trying to be Job-like has gone out of the window.

Nightline focused on the stifling of voices in the wake of the tragedy. After a fine report by one of its reporters, Ted Koppel convened a roundtable to discuss how the tragedy has caused journalists to be careful.

I turned to my wife and said, "God, I hope there are some black journalists on this roundtable." Her response? "Yea, right."

Yep, she was right. We were treated to three white guys – including a Texas columnist who was fired for criticizing the president – and a white woman. Again, no diversity of thought or opinion on this subject.

You name it, there has been some white guy talking about how this tragedy affects America. The subjects are so varied: terrorism, biochemical attacks, safety, transportation, Islam, Christianity, intelligence and racial profiling.

Attempts have been made by several outlets to mix up their talking heads.

About the only person who consistently has supported diverse viewpoints has been Bill Maher and his show *Politically Incorrect*. At least he has been on his game. But as a whole, the industry has not done well. I have personally communicated with black reporters and producers at several networks who have privately complained that they are having difficulty in getting their respective booking departments to include more black, Hispanic and Asian sources.

There have been a plethora of stories from college campuses regarding this issue, but have you seen a report from a historically black college campus?

I don't want to see the black angle. It would simply be nice to see such a campus being chosen as the source of a report.

I viewed a network report on what Christian ministers were saying about the attack. Guess what? Three white guys. Yes, Bishop T.D. Jakes and the

85

Speak, Brother!

president's spiritual adviser, the Rev. Kirbyjon Caldwell, have gotten some face time. But it has still been unequal.

We have seen damn near every person who used to serve in a presidential Cabinet being interviewed. But it's amazing that people like former transportation secretary Rodney Slater, former labor secretary Alexis Herman, former United Nations Ambassador Donald McHenry, former assistant secretary of state Susan Rice, former secretaries of the Army Togo West and Clifford Alexander, and so many others have not been seen. Hell, the current U.S. Surgeon General, Dr. David Satcher, is a brother, yet we keep seeing other folks talk about the mental health of America! Can we at least see the nation's top doc discuss this issue? Noted psychologist Dr. Alvin Poussaint has also been noticeably quiet, and I'm sure not by his own choosing.

It's not hard to find such sources. The week of the attack, I was on the *Tom Joyner Morning Show* and nearly all of these folks I've mentioned were interviewed. Then again, Joyner is a nationally syndicated morning show host who has a predominantly black audience. He's made the effort to have their phone numbers.

Let's get some other names on the table. ABC, to their credit, had poet Maya Angelou on Sept. 14, and she was so wonderful! But aside from appearing on *Oprah*, she hasn't been seen since. Andrew Young is a former big city mayor and ambassador to the United Nations who has extensive experience dealing with the Israeli-Palestinian conflict (he lost his UN job after it was reported he was meeting secretly with Palestinians). He also was one of the co-chairs of a commission that released a detailed report on the threat of terrorism in America earlier this year. I recall only seeing him on the day of the national prayer service.

Dr. Cornel West of Harvard and Dr. Michael Eric Dyson are two wonderful voices that could speak on the religious issue. Have they been on the boob tube? Hardly.

Roger Ferguson, the number two official at the Federal Reserve, was the person who quickly stabilized the financial markets in the aftermath of the attacks because his boss, Alan Greenspan, was out of the country. Has anyone given him credit for moving so fast and tried to talk with him?

Each network has former military officers as experts. Yet I cannot recall seeing a single African American in this position. Not one! Ladies and gents, what gives?

Nearly every person serving on the Senate and House intelligence committees have been talked to. But I don't recall seeing Rep. Alcee Hastings of Florida and Rep. Sanford Bishop of Georgia being asked their opinion on the perceived breakdown in intelligence.

Top editors at *Fortune* and *Forbes* have been mainstays on the business shows regarding the turbulence in the financial markets. Don't you think the folks at *Black Enterprise* are equally adept at discussing such issues?

Speak, Brother!

Airline pilots were sought out when stories emerged about cockpit safety. But did anyone reach out to the Organization of Black Airline Pilots? They even lost one of their own – Leroy Homer was one of the pilots of the United flight that crashed in Pennsylvania.

Many columnists have been interviewed on a number of roundtables. But where is James Campbell of the *Houston Chronicle*, the *Miami Herald's* Leonard Pitts, Bette Baye of the *Louisville Courier-Journal*, Gannett's DeWayne Wickham, Derrick Jackson of the *Boston Globe*, and Rochelle Riley of the *Detroit Free Press*? (If you want a list of other black columnists go to www.trottergroup.com).

I know some of my non-black colleagues may see this as a call for quotas and me being far too sensitive on this issue. If so, they miss the point. This is simply about journalists and news executives doing their job and doing what is right.

As long as we continue to see mostly white faces, we will not be able to further the conversation and open up the floor for different viewpoints and perspectives on this terrible and senseless tragedy.

Then again, I guess the lack of diverse voices shows that at least the American media has returned to normal.

Somebody has to look out for the little people

Oct. 24. 2001

Members of the U.S. House of Representatives took a big hit last week when they decided to adjourn for five days to allow federal health officials to sweep their office buildings for signs of anthrax.

Far too many blowhards in the media, as well as the House's compadres in the Senate, took them to task, saying they were sending the wrong message. They felt that America's political leaders should be sticking their chests out and showing the terrorists that their actions would not disrupt the nation's business. We were all treated to senators and their staffs crammed into small rooms as the television cameras rolled to show them passing legislation and doing "the people's work."

Oh, how silent the critics have fallen after more anthrax contamination was discovered in congressional office buildings, as well as the news of postal workers dying and being infected with the deadly disease. It didn't bother me to see them close up shop – lives are too precious to unnecessarily take such risks in order to score political points.

There is little doubt that the terrorists who have decided to strike America want to destroy our institutions as much as they can. But there comes a time when political leaders must not prove how macho they are, and instead, focus on the lives of thousands of unknown and low-paid workers in and around the nation's capitol.

It must be duly noted that the letters laced with anthrax did not infect Sen. Thomas Daschle, D-S.D., NBC's Tom Brokaw, CBS's Dan Rather or any of the other big name folks who they were mailed to. Instead, it was the lowly workers in the mailroom who are bearing the brunt on the attack.

These are people we are not used to seeing on our televisions and in our newspapers. These men and women – black, brown, white, American, immigrant, Republican, Democrat, conservative and liberal – are the folks who really drive the engine known as the federal government. If they stop working, then the nation's business will truly come to a standstill.

I would surmise that this is the reason House members chose not to continue working. Why risk continued infections, and potential deaths, in an effort to prove to others that they can withstand the bioterrorism attacks and continue their work?

What is more shameful than the initial reaction from columnists, cartoonists and talk radio hosts is their failure to apologize for their behavior and admit that the House decision was a just one. But then again, getting the media to apologize is about as likely as getting Al Gore to admit that he blew it by not using Bill Clinton enough in the presidential election.

Speak, Brother!

In the wake of the September 11 attack, some parts of America seem to be willing to take unnecessary and costly risks in the name of showing our resolve. I believe the military action in Afghanistan is doing just that, along with the surge in patriotism that has been borne out of the attack.

There's no sense in losing thousands more by forcing people to work in potential death zones just to make a point.

What will America do now?

Oct. 29, 2001

The news that federal law enforcement officials now believe that the anthrax attacks on the East Coast could likely be the result of U.S.-based terrorists should signal another wakeup to all Americans: don't be so quick to label just foreigners as terrorists.

The diabolical and hideous Sept. 11 attacks were still fresh in our minds when the entire United States police apparatus began to zero in on Osama bin Laden and individuals of Middle Eastern descent, rounding them up and putting them into custody. The moves were necessary as to ascertain who was responsible for the attacks that left more than 5,000 dead and nearly 10,000 wounded.

Despite pleas from Arab Americans to not racially-profile them, nearly everyone did just that. One poll even showed that 54 percent of African Americans favored profiling anyone looking like they were from the Middle East (And who better than black folks to understand the long-term and psychological effects of being a walking target).

"We didn't target white men with crew cuts," our Arab friends were heard to say, remarking on the failure to attack such folks after Timothy McVeigh – a former soldier of the United States military – planted a truck filled with explosives in 1995 and leveled the Alfred P. Murrah Federal Building in Oklahoma City, killing 169 people.

So what do we now as our law enforcement experts tell us that there are no links to bin Laden, and that "U.S. extremists" may be behind the anthrax scare? It would be simple to shrug that off and demand that more proof be offered. But so far, we have gone to great pains to trust the assumptions and hunches of the FBI and the CIA as it relates to this war. Why not this time?

I guess the real answers as to how we would respond lies in the fact that so few media outlets picked up on the story that was first reported in Saturday's Washington Post, which recounted the suspicions regarding who is behind the anthrax scare.

It is obvious that so many others can't fathom domestic terrorists doing such a horrible thing. But ask anyone who has been the victim of attacks from these armed militias, groups of largely white men from Idaho to Michigan who proclaim a deep love affair for America, yet at the same time they want to see the destruction of the country for what they consider to be its wayward ways.

And what are those ways? Among them: close ties to Israel and America's morals spiraling out of control. Hmmm...Don't they sound eerily familiar to the Islamic fundamentalists who we are supposed to be fighting? And what do these individuals call themselves? Defenders of the Christian faith. So one

91

Speak, Brother!

mans religious fanaticism is worthy of death while the other is met with silence from America.

These militia groups are filled with people who have hate running throughout their veins and are hell-bent on destroying the very fabric of this nation.

Much as the KKK of old, these so-called "Patriots" say they love this country yet they despite integration, immigration, multiculturalism and any non-Christian group. Far too many of them hide behind their heavily armored walls, stockpiling weapons as they wait on the next war. And unfortunately our own military government trained a significant number of them. And they could be your co-worker, next-door neighbor or even family member. Unlike the terrorists behind the Sept. 11 attack, these terrorists have blonde hair, blue eyes and have stiff backs when reciting the Pledge of Allegiance.

We all should wait with baited breath to see congressional and White House officials come out to call for a reward leading to the arrest and capture of these domestic terrorists. It has also crossed my mind as to whether President George W. Bush and others will call for the death of these individuals. Clearly there is precedent considering the spreading of anthrax has resulted in the deaths of three people and the infection of 18 others.

Murder is murder, whether with a gun, knife or mailing anthrax to the U.S. Capitol.

The anthrax scare is a real one. People are opening mail with masks and latex gloves, and keeping their children away from it all out of fear that they will contract the disease. The least our government can do is to continue to isolate all of the literature that has been mailed. And when that is done, use all the resources of the federal government and bring the perpetrators to justice, or as President Bush said of bin Laden, "Dead or alive."

Facing ones fears

Nov. 14, 2001

For the first time since September 11, I am scheduled to board an airplane and fly to New York tomorrow to assist in the closing of the February issue of *Savoy* Magazine. It would be a complete lie if I sat here and said I'm not thinking twice about doing so.

I knew the trip was coming up, and I was close to saying, "Okay, not a problem. You just move on like everyone says you should, hop on the plane, and pray all is well and go forward." Then I get a phone call at 9 a.m. Monday from BlackAmericaWeb.com's chief operating officer, Neil Foote, telling me – as I valiantly tried to wake up – that an American Airlines plane has gone down in New York, likely killing more than 250 people.

Goodbye, comfort zone. Hello, anxiety.

The devastation from September 11 and the aftermath have been difficult on so many others, including me. I was able to distance myself from the Oklahoma City bombing in 1995, even as I stood in front of the building for four days reporting on the carnage. The same goes for the countless hurricanes, tornadoes and fires I have covered over the years. But this was different. I knew it, yet it didn't hit me until a couple of weeks after. Now it takes everything I have just to be able to watch CNN.

As a newsman my job is to present the facts and avoid hype and emotion, yet who could not be affected by the indelible images of people jumping out of buildings, families losing mothers and fathers in an instant, and the nation we call home completely changed.

My minister says how can you quote Scripture, call yourself a Christian and say you're afraid to board a plane. My wife, an ordained minister, was comfortable when she boarded a plane two weeks ago to New Jersey to minister at a conference. But the hell with all of that macho stuff, I ain't afraid to say it: I'm scared.

I have gone into meditation on a continuous basis to seek guidance from God. I knew the answer before I even ventured into my prayer/meditation room at my home and conferred with my Lord. I felt good and safe in that quiet and peaceful sanctuary. Yet when that door opened and I was back in the real world, those worldly thoughts came rushing back.

I guess I'm writing these words to provide some sense of comfort to someone else out there who is seeking to move out of a perpetual freeze frame and go on. Maybe I'm also doing it to relieve me of the stress of flying, hoping this letter will act as a cathartic experience.

I know within the deep part of my soul that we must move on. As a child of God and a student of the Word, life must continue to evolve. Children will be born. Friends and relatives will go on to the Lord. Jobs will be switched. Our

Speak, Brother!

favorite sports team will win and lose. And terrible movies will continue to be made. I guess it's just a matter of having faith and resting and relying on Him.

Okay, enough straddling the fence and being indecisive. I'm ready to fly now.

Well, I still have 36 hours to change my mind...

He may be evil, but bin Laden is the Person of the Year

Dec. 24, 2001

By naming New York Mayor Rudy Giuliani it's Person of the Year, the current editorial staff of *Time* Magazine has thoroughly ignored the purpose of its year-end cover story, which formerly was the Man of the Year, and has abdicated its responsibility to uphold the legacy of Henry Luce.

When Luce first conceived the idea in 1925, it was to recognize ``the person who most affected the news or our lives, for good or for ill, this year.''

Time managing editor Jim Kelly said Giuliani was the choice "because of his courage on Sept. 11 and afterwards, because a very human man showed superhuman strengths at a time when the entire country was being tested. He showed the way out of our despair, and gave us the emotional armor to get up every day and get on with our lives. He led by emotion, not just by words and actions, and in an emotional year like this one, he deserved to be our Person of the Year."

Of bin Laden, Kelly was obviously less than doting. "And though we spent hours debating the pros and cons of naming Osama bin Laden, it ultimately became easy to dismiss him. He is not a larger than life figure with broad historical sweep; as the tapes showed, he is smaller than life, a garden-variety terrorist whose evil plan succeeded beyond his highest hopes and who is now either dead or running for his life."

But the reality is were it not for the heinous acts committed by those loyal to bin Laden, Rudy would have never shown that.

Choosing bin Laden as the Person of the Year would have, as some suggested, been a marketing mess for *Time*. But that should not have been the overriding concern. This is a matter of history, not subscribers. The actions of killing 3,000 people have arguably had a generational and potentially longer impact on Americans.

Are we a different country today because of Rudy's leadership? No. I surmise that a number of big city mayors would have responded just the same. But has our attitude and psyche been forever changed because of the attacks on the World Trade Center and the Pentagon? Absolutely yes.

The attacks have led Americans to question everything about us, our nation and our role as the world's lone superpower. It has even brought out the worst in Americans, namely the massive racial profiling that has resulted. We think twice about air travel because of the uncertainty, which will surely return after the report of a Sri Lanka man having explosives in his athletic shoes aboard an international flight bound for Miami. Marriages are on the increase. More people became pregnant. A lot of people resigned from jobs to focus more on their family or to live out a lifelong dream. Life insurance jumped dramatically. All of this a result of what took place on Sept. 11.

Speak, Brother!

Although he isn't saying it, *Time's* Jim Kelly didn't want his first choice as Person of the Year to lead to thousands of cancellations and spending an eternity in defending the choice of bin Laden. But Time has been there before. Hitler, Joseph Stalin and Ayatollah Khomeini have been designated before, and not a one of them was a well-liked guy.

Despite Giuliani and others proclaiming it as an honor to be chosen, it is not the Academy Award of journalism.

Sorry, *Time*. The media juggernaut in New York has already given Rudy G. his props for the response after Sept. 11. You chose to take the safe route, instead of upholding the legacy and purpose for which Luce created the Person (Man) of the Year.

SECTION FIVE
SPORTS

Was I a football player? Why would you ask that?

Sept. 9, 1994

As my beloved Texas A&M Aggies strap on the pad and helmets for another victorious season in the soon-to-be-deceased Southwest Conference, I must also put on my game face for the unbearable number of times I will be asked the question: "Did you play football?

People I don't even know let those four words roll off their tongues with ease, not knowing the impact they have.

Whether I am at a reception or at the clothing store looking to buy a maroon blazer to wear to Aggie games, the moment someone learns that I went to A&M – either by asking or looking at my Aggie ring – they always ask the question.

Most of the time I politely say "no." On a few rare occasions, I have walked away without saying a word.

Some may consider me a wee bit sensitive. But I understand that the people who ask that question only see two things: a thick African-American man who went to a predominantly white school.

Presto! Gotta be a ballplayer.

With the prestige, name identification and reverence we give athletes, many people probably would be overjoyed if someone mistook them for a big-time college athlete.

But after spending hundreds of hours studying and thousand of dollars on books, food and aspirin during my 4 1/2 –year college career, it is nauseating to be reduced to a stereotype.

As a child growing up in Houston, my mom and dad never really encourage me and my four siblings to play sports. My older brother played baseball in high school and was in the band. I also limited my extracurricular activities to those two endeavors.

My dad wanted education to be a priority, as opposed to going through life with a "dumb jock" label attached. But we somehow can't escape the trap.

Instead of people giving us the chance to attend college *without* an athletic scholarship, we get lumped into a category that somehow always applies to African-American men.

We live in a world where race is pervasive and labels are attached to everyone. Italian-Americans can't get away from the mafia image; people from Arab countries are always portrayed as mad terrorists; Irish-Americans are considered drunken bigots; and Asian Americans are always labeled as smart.

And, of course, African-American men play ball.

Although we laugh at these jokes in comedy clubs, these portrayals, when applied in real life, unmercifully hurt those who are the targets.

99

Speak, Brother!

I've always been cognizant of other people's feelings when I meet them. I don't automatically assume that a very tall man who went to a major college or university played basketball.

When I'm on the golf course and I see someone rip the ball nearly 300 yards, my first impression isn't that he played golf in college.

I've made many people feel horribly guilty because they assumed I was a ballplayer. It has crossed my mind that I shouldn't do that. But maybe that person, the next time he or she meets an African-American man, will think about how they insulted me by jumping to a conclusion.

I may not be able to solve this country's infatuation with race and stereotypes, but I can certainly knock down one barrier on the road to another.

Sir Charles, you are way out of line

March 9, 2002

For years we have come to expect a number of things from Charles Barkley, least of which is that his mouth will always match his girth.

But seeing him on the cover of *Sports Illustrated* dressed as if he were a slave, albeit with broken chains, was a little too much to handle from the anti-role model.

Since retiring from the NBA, Barkley has continued to amaze fans with his constantly moving mouth, pontificating on subjects ranging from racism in golf to why Michael Jordan should not have returned to the game to the sorry state of the NBA today. He has been slapped on the back for his candidness, and critics have called him a breath of fresh air for his no-holds-barred style.

Charles, we'll give you your props for irreverent commentary on TNT, but as for some of the idiotic statements you continue to make, as well as that hideous SI cover, you're simply an asinine ass who needs to know and understand that some subjects are beyond your ridicule. As a friend of mine put it: would a Jew dress in dowdy clothes, stand behind a barbed wire fence and stick his head out of an oven? Fat chance.

Charles Barkley may have $30 million in the bank, play golf five times a week and pal around with his boy, Michael Jordan, but his understanding of the depth of slavery on America's psyche shows that he didn't pay much attention during history class.

There is no institution in the history of this country that is as wretched as the slave trade. Although so many of us – black and white – have been exposed to the truths of slavery through a few television shows like Roots and various documentaries, the destruction of a people is hard to fathom in a country supposedly built on independence and freedom.

We cannot lose sight of the fact that while Barkley mocks a slave, real men, women and children were exposed to such indignities, and they weren't wearing pristine white pants and faking a menacing look on their face. Instead, the look on their faces likely were borne from the pain and agony of being torn from their families and homeland, forced to endure the smell of death across the Atlantic Ocean, then the humiliating and disgraceful practice of being sold to the highest bidder and sent to work in hot fields under the dictatorship of a white slave master.

Our imaginations cannot fathom our beautiful black queens being raped and pilloried by their masters, and all the African men could do was to sit in silence, their rage boiling underneath their tired and listless bodies. Who can forget the stories of slaves being beaten for simply trying to read or write.

101

Speak, Brother!

These are not stories derived from a Hollywood writer, but true accounts of the conditions of slaves on plantations in Alabama, Mississippi, Tennessee, Georgia, Virginia and so many other places.

Even when the Emancipation Proclamation was signed and the era of Reconstruction was ushered in, the ancestors of Africans were forced to work as sharecroppers – another form of slavery.

Years passed, and while the label "free" was attached to us all, Jim Crow made sure black folks continued to live under the oppressive white hand of evil. We went through the Civil Rights Movement, the Black Power Movement, the Black Bourgeoisie Movement and every other kind of movement, yet while so many of us have "made it," others are still locked in the system that is the byproduct of slavery.

Charles Barkley proclaims that he's a free man, yet even he frets about there being no black owners of any professional sports league, and that the good ol' boy network is at work in the NBA.

What gets my blood boiling isn't just his trifling pose as a slave, but also the insistence of the editors of *Sports Illustrated* to use this quote as the major tease on its cover: "Every black kid thinks the only way he can be successful is through athletics. That is a terrible thing."

A terrible thing? No, a terrible thing is to put this quote on the cover as some social statement from a wanna-be social critic for a bunch of black boys and girls to read. The problem in America isn't that black kids want to be athletes or entertainers so they can have their big cribs, large rides and sexual escapades explored on *MTV Cribs* and in *People* Magazine. What our dear friends in the media fail miserably at is giving us consistent images of brothers and sisters who have made millions by working in technology, business, aerospace, construction and countless other professions.

If young black America is fed a constant diet of hip-hop ads showing Alan Iverson drenched in diamonds, Michael Jordan gliding through the air with the chorus singing, "Want to be like Mike," and Kobe knocking down millions in endorsements, who in the hell does Barkley or SI think these cats will want to emulate?

It's not as if *Sports Illustrated* has made its mission to consistently show the black athlete in a position other than slam dunking, being absent fathers or in handcuffs. How about this SI: Since your bread-and-butter is showcasing the amazing skills of mostly black athletes, why haven't you tapped one of the many talented black men and women as the top editor of your magazine? Now that's something we can show to young black kids and say, "If you handle your business, you don't have to get in SI by running the ball. You can determine what stories get run in *Sports Illustrated*." I'll try not to hold my breath for your reply to that one.

Speak, Brother!

Charles Barkley the basketball player is one of the NBA's 50 Greatest Players. But as a social commentator, he is just about as effective as a comedian occupying the White House.

Sir Charles, you've done what you set out to accomplish. We're all talking about you and your name is in headlines. But take that knowledge you love to tell others to get and put it to use: slavery is no joke. You are.

Tyrone, tell Notre Dame to go to hell

Dec. 14, 2001

Neo-classic soul singer Erykah Badu made famous the phrase, "I think you better call Tyrone." In the wake of George O'Leary resignation as head coach at Notre Dame for lying on his resume, many are suggesting the school call Stanford's Tyrone Willingham and hire him as coach of the Fighting Irish.

If I'm Willingham and that phone rings and Notre Dame athletic director Kevin White is on the other line, he would be greeted with three words: "Go to hell!"

When Notre Dame fired Bob Davie after five lackluster seasons, Willingham was one of the top names on their wish list.

The storied Fighting Irish program had completely been demoralized during Davie's tenure, and the school was desperately trying to restore it to the elite status of college football.

The Fighting Irish wanted NFL coaches like Oakland's Jon Gruden and Steve Mariucci of the San Francisco 49'ers, but they declined. The school asked Stanford if they could interview Willingham and they were given permission.

But Notre Dame never even set up an interview, another case of window dressing. All too often schools and even professional teams have put a black candidate on the list, give them a courtesy interview – if that – and then quickly scratch their name off the list to move to the next person.

So Notre Dame turned to Georgia Tech's George O'Leary, a decent coach who led his team to five straight bowl games. Not a big deal these days when you can have an average season and get a bid to the galleryfurniture.com Bowl. The man never even won his own conference title, which is sort of a barometer for hiring qualified coaches, especially at Notre Dame.

He was described as the perfect fit; a man of integrity who would be focused on winning and graduating athletes.

Now, five days later, O'Leary is out a job because he lied on his resume.

It seems the media did what Notre Dame didn't think about doing: going over his bio to see if he did do what he said he did. The 55-year-old O'Leary said he earned a master's degree from New York University in 1972. Lie! He said he lettered for three years in football at New Hampshire. Lie! He didn't even earn one letter and worse, never played in a single game.

"Due to a selfish and thoughtless act many years ago, I have personally embarrassed Notre Dame, its alumni and fans," O'Leary said in a statement.

"The integrity and credibility of Notre Dame is impeccable and with that in mind, I will resign my position as head football coach," he said. His resignation was effective Thursday.

Speak, Brother!

Notre Dame fans are now shaking their heads, wondering what in the heck happened and school officials are thoroughly embarrassed. As a result, the attention is now turning back to Willingham, who is now being called the best candidate for the job.

Tyrone Willingham was the best candidate before Notre Dame hired O'Leary, and he's a standup guy with impeccable credentials and a strong command of the game.

Does he have a sparkling record? No, but what black college coach in Division I-A does? Typically, the schools that give a black coach a chance are at the bottom of the barrel or in conferences where they are guaranteed to have a terrible season after season. Out of 117 schools in Division I-A, only four have a black head coach. They are at weak programs like Michigan State (Bobby Williams), New Mexico State (Tony Samuel) and San Jose State (Fitz Hill). A fifth, Jerry Baldwin, was fired by Louisiana-Lafayette.

Willingham, a former NFL assistant coach, has led Stanford to a 44-35-1 record and his team is 9-2 this year. He has run a solid program at a school that puts academics before anything else, and has done so with integrity.

But like so many other black coaches, Willingham is never seriously considered for the big-time jobs when they become available. It would be unthinkable for non-blacks, even with us heading into 2002, to see a black coach stalking the sidelines at Miami, Florida State, UCLA, USC, Alabama and Texas. The school administrators wouldn't even interview them, and if they did, fans and alumni wouldn't stand for it.

Athletics is supposed to be all about who is the best skilled. Can you throw the ball better than the man standing next to you? Good, you're the quarterback. Can you stop the run? Perfect, you're our middle linebacker. That's what coaches tell their athletes, so why can't school administrators use the same barometer when choosing coaches?

Tyrone Willingham is a class act that should have been treated better by Notre Dame. Now some want him to get sloppy seconds. If I'm him, I'm saying, "No thanks. You said he was the perfect fit now he isn't. If I get the job, how will you introduce me at the news conference? 'Here's the second-best man for the job on our list?'"

One prominent sportscaster told me that if he were Willingham he would schedule an interview, go through the motions, wait until the school offered the job and scheduled a news conference, and then tell them no thanks. That's kind of vindictive, but certainly deserving for a school that says one thing and then does another.

Maybe the best thing is to simply tell Notre Dame's White that the days of pimping black coaches have ended.

Jim Brown doesn't deserve our sympathy

April 17, 2002

NFL Hall of Fame running back Jim Brown sits in a California jail, refusing to eat in order to protest the treatment he has received after a judge ordered him to attend counseling after being found guilty of damaging his wife's car in a 1999 domestic dispute.

Presenting himself as an example of a criminal justice system that denigrates, destroys and dismantles black men, the 66-year-old Brown says he will not allow his manhood to be taken away during the six-month jail term he received.

"You cannot take my dignity...," Brown said after being sentenced. "Fifteen years, 20 years, 27 years Nelson Mandela spent to fight apartheid in South Africa. Only that man did it."

Did I miss something? Nelson Mandela fought for apartheid to end. Brown is in jail for refusing to do community service work and attend counseling. That's not even a close comparison.

Unfortunately, his pathetic attempt to be seen as the victim has been picked up by some black writers who have interviewed him. They have written sympathetic stories, trying to rally the masses to come to his side in a show of solidarity.

Thanks, Jim. But black America has been pimped long enough by well-known blacks that have misguided motives when they are clearly in the wrong.

Jim Brown is undoubtedly the finest running back professional football has ever seen. He is number two all-time in career rushing yards and is the standard by which every running back is measured. He was tough, brutal and downright intimidating when the ball was tucked underneath his arm. After leaving the NFL after only nine seasons, he has garnered the respect of many for his work to end gang violence, as well as an outspoken advocate of social change within the sports world.

But there is an intimidating side of Jim Brown that too many don't want to focus on. He has had a number of legal issues over the years that relate to domestic violence. He was accused of throwing one woman out of a second story window, and in this latest case, his wife called 911 after Brown blew up and began to destroy her car. During the call she intimated that he had physically assaulted her in the past. Many of the cases against Brown didn't go to trial because the women recanted.

A man is innocent until proven guilty. But those who study domestic violence know full well that women who have been abused often refuse to testify, leading prosecutors to drop the case because the key witness won't take the stand.

Speak, Brother!

Brown maintains that he had a right to attack his wife's car and beat it to a pulp, telling a USA Today writer that they teach in anger management classes that you should hit something else instead of your spouse. How about this Jim: Can you learn to not hit anything by controlling your anger?

The statistics on domestic abuse are sobering. Thousands of women are abused, some even killed, by men who don't know how to control their anger (And there are cases where men are physically abused by women). Their girlfriends and wives are treated as human punching bags by these men who are raging lunatics, often after they have been drinking or doing drugs.

O.J. Simpson and Ike Turner have become the poster children for domestic violence. But men who are CEO's, politicians, police officers, lawyers and blue-collar workers, regardless of color, are also guilty of domestic violence. It is a sad and troubling issue that must be stopped by those women prosecuting the men in their lives, as well as family members and friends not turning the other cheek when it happens.

No one – and I mean no one – should dare take up Jim Brown's cause. He is not a role model. His stance is not one that we should be proud of. And he is flat out wrong for trying to manipulate the media by casting himself as the victim.

What Jim Brown needs to do is take a long hard look at himself in the mirror. Instead of spending his time on a hunger strike, Brown should use the 23 hours a day he spends alone in his jail cell to take a self-analysis of who he is and what has happened in his life that causes the angry side of him to erupt.

Jim, I respect you for what you did on the football field and for what you have accomplished to end gang violence. But you get no love when it comes to physically abusing women. It's time for you to end your troubling history of domestic violence.

The ball's in your hands.

Barry Bonds and the problem with raising the race issue

Nov. 20, 2001

There is little doubt that racism is so deeply embedded in the American psyche that it's hard to fathom anyone possessing the opinion that it no longer is alive in America.

Dredging up the disgusting murder of James Byrd at the hand of three hate-filled white men in Jasper, Texas, could be cited as enough evidence. How about the killing of five unarmed black men by Cincinnati police officers, all of whom weren't convicted of their heinous crime? Or what about the tale of a black CEO, whose company did $6 billion in transactions last year? According to the December issue of *Savoy* Magazine, Owen May and a friend, dressed in jeans, golf shirts and sneakers, went to the offices of the real estate brokerage firm of Insignia/ESG to find some new office space after losing everything in the World Trade Center attack. An executive of the firm looked at May and asked if he was making a delivery. Yes, racism is so alive that it permeates every institution of this country – judicial, electoral, financial and educational.

But there are times when race is not always at the heart of an issue.

And that's what brings us to Barry Bonds.

The San Francisco Giants outfielder is coming off the best homerun season in the history of Major League Baseball, smashing 73 homeruns to break the record of Mark McGwire. The record, along with his overall play, led Bonds to win his record fourth National League MVP in a 16-year career.

He has a high wattage smile, comes from a lineage that includes a father who played in the big leagues and a godfather who was a pretty good player in his day, Willie Mays. So why isn't Barry setting records for endorsements?

According to the rules of the "system," an athlete who makes an unmistakable mark on the sport he plays always finds himself cashing in on advertising contracts. McGwire picked up $5 million in deals after he broke the homerun record several years ago. Sammy Sosa, who was in the hunt with Big Mac, is believed to have gotten more. No one has more endorsements than Tiger Woods and Michael Jordan, yet virtually no advertisers are falling at the feet of Bonds to lavish him with riches.

Life has changed since Sept. 11, but it hasn't changed that much. A significant number of African Americans have charged that the rules have been changed at that Bonds is not getting his due because he is black.

Can you say hogwash?

The exhibition Barry Bonds has put on this year has been absolutely awesome. But his record-breaking feats notwithstanding, Barry Bonds has been a surly ass much of his career. I'm not one speaking from what I heard, but from what I know.

Speak, Brother!

While covering a game three years ago between the Texas Rangers and the Giants, I ventured into the locker room to interview Bonds and several other players. But talking to him was a complete waste of time as he was rude, spaced out and absolutely a waste of my time. If you read the horror stories from Bay Area reporters, they can tell you of an athlete who is considered selfish, obnoxious, standoffish and downright moody – and that's what his fellow players say!

I do not subscribe to the belief that an athlete must kiss the butt of every member of the media in order to get the respect he richly deserves or to cash in on the riches from the advertising community. There are many of my media brethren who are pathetic themselves. But like it or not, we all know that the media plays a large role in how an athlete is perceived.

One of the reasons we wrap ourselves in the lore of athlete's in yesteryear is because of the rich reporting by sports scribes of their amazing accomplishments. MJ isn't considered "The Man" all because of his game on the court. He also represented an ideal athlete: well spoken, not harsh with words, available for interviews. Charles Barkley is an athlete who was boorish, loud and could be downright rude. But Sir Charles would give you a laugh after cussing you out, and all you would be left with is, "That's Charles!"

Barry Bonds will not get a chance to sit at the advertisers/sponsors buffet and make out like players in the past. He'll have to be content with the $10 million he made last season.

Don't waste a second trying to come to Bonds' defense as another black man who is a victim of "the system." It has nothing to do with his skin being darkened by the kiss of the sun, but more to do with the image he cultivated in 15 previous seasons, rather than the magic he performed in the latest.

Never hold your tongue, Nolan

March 1, 2002

Malcolm X once said that the man you should be most afraid of is one who isn't afraid to die. In 2002, thank goodness we have men like Nolan Richardson who are willing to lay it all on the line – even if the price is a high-paying job – to speak the cold hard truth when it comes to race.

Richardson, the successful Arkansas men's head basketball coach, is on the brink of losing his job because he went public with his personal feelings on the thorny subject. That has unsettled the Arkansas faithful and administration, and has led them to privately form a search committee to replace him.

Richardson, never one to hold his tongue in the more than two decades he has coached, blasted the school's fans and media, saying he is being treated differently because he is a black coach.

"See, my great-great-grandfather came over on the ship, I didn't," he said. "I didn't come on that ship, so I expect to be treated a little bit different."

"Because I know for a fact that I do not play on the same level as the other coaches around this school play on," he continued. "I know that. You know it. And people of my color know that. And that angers me."

Here are some other Richardson comments:

Social life in Fayetteville. Black athletes come to the school just to "play basketball or come to play football."

Graduation rates. Doesn't believe the responsibility solely falls to the coach, saying the parents should focus on that.

His legacy. "Sometimes you can be crucified as you leave, but feeling this crucifix is wonderful to me inside because I was sent here to do a job...my presence in those institutions made it a better place for people to live and respect. They know I wasn't an Uncle Tom."

On the media covering his team. "When I look at all of you people in this room, I see no one that looks like me, talks like me or acts like me. Now, why don't you recruit? Why don't the editors recruit like I'm recruiting?"

School chancellor John White, seething at the comments, has said they have set the program back – whatever in the hell that means – and will meet with Richardson to resolve the issues. White's dim view of Richardson's comments goes to show you that he is clueless to the real and raw emotions of the man who has led the school to a national championship (1994), three Final Four appearances, totaled a 389-169 record in 17 years (508-226 in 22 totals years of college coaching), and 14 appearances in the NCAA tournament.

"So what can you take away from me?" Richardson asked. "I've won everything there is to win. Name me coaches that can say that."

Speak, Brother!

Even the state's governor, Mike Huckabee, has come to Nolan's defense, saying that he has overcome a lot. "That's one of the things that a lot of people now don't fully comprehend," Huckabee said.

"They haven't walked in his shoes. They haven't taken his journey. They may not fully understand some of the deep feelings that he carries inside. There's a wonderful success story in Nolan Richardson."

The Arkansas school newspaper, *The Arkansas Traveler*, came to his defense in an editorial on Friday.

"For 17 years, Nolan put this university on the map. Bud Walton Arena was built for him, and he christened it with a National Championship banner," the paper wrote. "Though he might have not expressed himself very well off the court Monday, the banners in Bud Walton Arena speak volumes.

"Nolan deserves to be the coach as long as he wants to, which, hopefully, will be long enough to hang another National Champion banner here."

Some have suggested that Richardson, who makes $1 million a year, should just shut up, take his lump sum payment of $3 million, walk away and land a job at another high-profile Division I-A school. Critics have said that other coaches have been fired and ridden off into the sunset. But such comments are shortsighted and don't speak to the heart of the issues Richardson has raised. The man has spent a third of his life at the school and is being pushed out the door.

Arkansas, without a doubt, is having a bad season. The team is 13-14 overall and 5-10 in the Southeastern Conference. But one tough season cannot wipeout all the success that he has had. Yet fans in Arkansas are fickle. They want Nolan's head on a platter no matter what.

A man of his credentials and integrity is being pushed around unnecessarily, and seemingly forced out by an administration that is willing to cede to the demands of a faithful few alumni and hang Richardson out to dry.

His comments about race being a factor in all of this are on the money. He knows it, school administrators know it and many of the fans know it. If you want to talk about performance on the court then there is no question they can't touch Richardson. So what else is there?

Nolan Richardson has been a boon to college athletics, and black coaches in particular, because he has refused to accept the status quo and live on the golf course while pocketing a hefty paycheck.

He deserves to stay as coach, be left alone by the administrators and fans, and continue to build his legacy.

If John Wooden continues to reign supreme at UCLA, Ray Meyer is hailed as Mr. DePaul basketball and the uncompromising bigot Adolph Rupp is still revered in Kentucky, then surely the Arkansas faithful can give Richardson his just due.

He has earned it.

Switzer has priorities in order

Oct. 2, 1994

As a youngster playing baseball in Houston, my mom and dad didn't get to attend many of my baseball games.

While I cherished the moments they were in the stands to see their second son play, I understood my mom working a day shift and my dad at night, all to feed and clothe our family of seven.

So it was with great respect and admiration when I heard that Barry Switzer took Jerry Jones' private plane the night before the Cowboys played the Houston Oilers to go see his son play a game in Missouri.

And it was with anger when I heard Jimmy Johnson, the coach who was booking to get out of Dallas but who seems to miss the team more than ever, criticize Switzer for placing his family first.

I shouldn't have expected anything less from a man who left his wife and children because he wanted to devote all of his time and energy to winning football games.

Priorities, priorities.

Football coaches have always gotten the rap of being obsessive, driven and determined egomaniacs that will go to any length to win games. The pressure and high stakes that go along with coaching a professional sports team has driven many coaches to retire their clipboard and polyester pants.

John Madden had to get out of Oakland when his heart couldn't stand it. Dick Vermeil, whom many considered one of the most intense coaches to walk the sidelines, almost drove himself crazy with the long hours and pressure to win. And Joe Gibbs, often sleeping on his office couch after putting in 20 hours a day at the office, left a successful and high-paying job with the Redskins to spend more time with his family.

While other forces may have also led to these men leaving the game, spending time with a wife and family has been one of the major reasons for leaving the profession.

But the obsessiveness exhibited by coaches isn't exclusive to that fraternity.

We live in a society where our individual career goals are often placed before brothers, sisters, wives and parents.

The need for the $200,000 house, the latest luxury car and vacations in Rome and the Caribbean has caused many people to forget about the value of a loving family.

I don't have any kids, but I appreciate seeing my little cousins grow up and become young men and women. It is unforgettable to watch moments like the high school or college graduation of a loved one.

Speak, Brother!

Whenever there is a lull in my life or things are getting too hectic, my mind always reverts back to the crazy things my brother and I used to do, as well as the butt-whippings we got for our mischievous deeds.

So it is understandable that Switzer wouldn't want to miss seeing his son playing football.

There might have been a number of times when Switzer was at the University of Oklahoma when he missed his son running down the sidelines in the Pop Warner League. Maybe he missed the high school game where his son threw a winning touchdown pass in the waning moments of the game.

Watching the highlights on film is nothing compared to having your stomach wrench with pain as you hope and pray – especially with thousands of cheering fans waiting to hail or curse your child – that Junior hits that wide receiver across the back of the end zone.

Switzer could have been there to see his son play, but maybe he wasn't. Maybe Switzer, thinking his son won't go to the pros, is trying to see those last plays with his own eyes.

Barry Switzer owes no apology to anyone for going to see his son play. Sure, he doesn't want to see his personal life conflict with his professional one. But sometimes that is a choice we all have to make.

Jimmy Johnson may not have given a damn about those times with his wife and family, times that can never be repeated.

But hopefully many rabid sports fans, especially all the men who plop down in front of their TV sets on Sunday, will follow Switzer's example and understand the value of your permanent family over your football family.

SECTION SIX
MEDIA

Liberating Black America Through Mass Media

Jan. 21, 2002

Speech given at The Rev. Martin Luther King Jr. annual luncheon, sponsored by the Phi Chapter of Alpha Phi Alpha Fraternity, Inc., at Ohio University.

Knowing full well that the kingdom of God is the greatest of any institution in this world, let me say that there is no greater institution of this world than the mass media. I'll repeat that for those who didn't hear me: there is no greater institution in this world than the mass media. Some have said that the president of the United States is the most powerful man in the world. Yet history tells that Presidents Richard Nixon and Bill Clinton, among others, were brought to their knees as a result of the relentless media pressure against them for their actions in the Oval Office. The media can build you up or tear you down. The media can make you're an overnight sensation or it can cast you aside like a bubble gum wrapper. Andy Warhol said fame last 15 minutes, yet depending on who you tick off, the media can turn that fame into infamy.

Just think back for a few seconds. Were it not for the coalescing of media interests, more than $1 billion dollars could not have been raised for victims of the Sept. 11 terrorist attack. Were it not for the intense media coverage, none of us would have been aware of some of the terrorists living next door to us.

We stand here to honor Martin Luther King Jr. for his historic works to this world, yet many of us don't realize that prior to the fire hoses being turned on little black boys and girls in Alabama, much of the country regarded the Civil Rights Movement as a Negro Movement and not an American Movement. When those televised pictures were shown all around the country white America began to see the foul, flagrant and abusive attitudes of whites in the South, even though the struggle had been in full throttle for several years.

Just this past Friday we celebrated the 25th anniversary of the showing of *Roots*. Imagine had that show not been shown. What would have happened had Alex Haley not gone back to rediscover his past? Thousands of people – black, white and otherwise – would have not rediscovered their roots and gotten in contact with their fellow relatives across the country. The showing of that one simple show changed the lives of millions of people. That is true power via the media.

Yet there is a downside to the media's influence. The media, or should we say the intense fight between media barons Joseph Pulitzer and William Randolph Hearst, is considered by many to be the first significant time that a fight to increase newspaper circulation led the United States to enter into a war.

Speak, Brother!

According to the television show *Yellow Journalism and the Spanish American War*, "For years before the Spanish/American War, William Randolph Hearst and Joseph Pulitzer had been fighting a battle for readership in the streets of New York City. By 1896, when Hearst arrived in New York to run his newspaper, *The New York Journal*, Pulitzer was enjoying great financial success by employing sensational reporting techniques that provided mass appeal. Hearst, not to be outdone, adopted similar tactics of yellow journalism to increase the circulation of his newspaper in an attempt to beat Pulitzer at his own game. In another aggressive tact, Hearst lured away journalists from Pulitzer's *New York World* by offering them unprecedented salaries. He also enticed some of the most talented nationally known artists, cartoonists and writers (including Ambrose Bierce and Mark Twain) to bolster readership of the Journal. But even these costly efforts did not afford him the success he desired.

"Both Hearst and Pulitzer perceived the impending war with Spain as the perfect subject matter to exploit. American patriotism was high and there was great interest in the events happening in Cuba. Hearst took special interest in the war, going so far as to personally edit all of the related stories. Likewise, Pulitzer ordered his journalists to stretch and distort the news. He chose to run stories that elaborated the most sordid, and violent details. Hearst and Pulitzer both dispatched journalists to cover the Cuban rebellion and the ensuing war. The reports that came back were often spun into hyperbolic stories, playing upon the fears and loyalties of the American public."

Their actions forced the federal government to engage in the war that last some 10 years and led the loss of thousands of lives. You tell me the media can't impact our lives to a large degree.

But we don't have to look at past history. I was reading a story the other day about how Texas-sized Western belt buckles are all the rage now. Why? Because rapper Jay-Z has started to wear them in videos, leading impressionable young minds to run to the store to copy his style. And who can forget the orthopedic style shoes being shown in a rap video leading to an overrun of the websites and phone lines of companies who made such shoes. No one older than 25 would have been caught dead in those shoes, yet because a rapper wore them in a video, all of a sudden they were the new rage.

Our minds have been shaped – for better or for worse – by what we see on television, in movies, listen to on the radio, watch in videos, observe on billboards, read in books, or the countless other forms of media.

There are those like the Pulitzers and Hearts who used the space in their newspapers to foster their own foreign policy, much like we see radio commentators like Rush Limbaugh or the conservative-leaning *Washington Times*, who choose to pump up the Republican Party and its ideals for their own self-serving interests. And we read liberal commentators who are more

Speak, Brother!

concerned with pushing Democratic Party ideals, even when they hurt those who they are intending to help.

In this quest for a liberated Black America through the mass media, we cannot help but laud the efforts of a Cathy Hughes, who took a small community-based radio station in Baltimore-Washington, D.C. named WOL and turned into a radio empire that is known as Radio One, the largest black-owned media company in the country. Yes, Radio One is now beholden to corporate shareholders, but it still maintains its focus of empowering the community.

But on the flip side, we have Bob Johnson, a man who used the grassroots effort to infiltrate and call upon black churches and politicians to demand that local cable companies carry his fledgling Black Entertainment Television more than 20 years ago. Yet today, BET is no longer black-owned, and it sure as hell has done little to cause a positive and substantive change in Black America.

Instead, we have been fed a diet of infomercials, shady and pathetic videos showing damn near butt-naked women and men – no, let me say boys – who belittle and denigrate these sisters, and uphold a lifestyle where all life is about is getting a big diamond encrusted cross with a rented Bentley and an expensive yet unfurnished house. Yes, BET has tried to have some informative and valuable content. But let me be clear: much of that has been inferior and downright shoddy, and certainly not quality television. I applaud Bob Johnson the businessman. I will not discredit what he has accomplished financially by becoming the first black billionaire. I will not dishonor the fact that for the first time in the history of black finance, a mainstream company has paid equal or greater value for a black-owned company. But I cannot dismiss the corrosive effect that BET has had on the collective conscious of Black America. Johnson has said that the "E" in BET stands for entertainment. I say it stands for egregious.

Some have said that BET is only showing what others will show and that they are only providing a service to these individuals who crave such information. But I be damned if I will allow my nieces, nephews and future children to ever say, "Dad, I'm selling drugs because there is a market and a demand for it and I'm just giving the public what they want." BET is not an addictive and illegal substance. But when you consider the kind of damaging information that is being shown on television it does have a negative effect on young impressionable minds because all they want to see and experience a lifestyle that we all know is not realistic at all.

When it comes to the liberation of Black America through the mass media, I can't help but think of strong willed brothers and sisters who have wanted to make money *and*, let me say it again, *and* be a strong influence on the conscious of America.

Speak, Brother!

I think of Ida B. Wells Barnett, a strong-willed sister from Holly Springs, Mississippi, who used her newspaper to rail against the widespread lynching of blacks throughout the South. Her newspaper was firebombed and a bounty was put on her head, yet Ida B. Wells Barnett did not allow any of that to still her tongue and fiery pen. John H. Johnson, as we all know is the founder of *Ebony* and *Jet*. We all must applaud Mr. Johnson's behavior – ain't it a shame that integrity doesn't go along with everyone who has the Johnson name? – in running his magazine. *Ebony* and *Jet* are both historic in that they have covered Black America – the good, the bad and the ugly. Last year Bryant Gumbel took a major shot at *Ebony* for showing big homes and celebrity lifestyles, yet such a statement completely ignores the historical impact that the magazine has had on Black America.

Can *Ebony* be better? Yes. Should more people buy *Jet* for the articles than the *Jet* Beauty of the Week? Absolutely. But *Ebony* and *Jet* have remained black-owned, despite the millions of dollars John J. Johnson could have reaped from selling his company. In an age where a handful of companies like Disney, Viacom, Time Warner, Clear Channel Communications, and Fox seem to own all of the major media properties, we all should be grateful that there is one company that is completely uncompromising in its mission to be an information source for Black America.

And the vital issue at hand is that simple 11-letter word: information. In the movie *Sneakers*, starring Sidney Poitier, Robert Redford and Ben Kingsley, there is a scene of the roof where Kingsley's character tells Redford's "you were so naïve. Information is the key to power and the future." If we don't know that an important bill on Capitol Hill could affect black America in a positive or negative fashion, then we can't do anything about it. If we don't know that Katz Media made a decision to tell advertisers not to buy time on black radio, then we couldn't expose them for the racists they were and expose the inherent and systematic racism that exists against black radio. I can stand here and tell countless stories and give you a litany of examples about how information and the ability to access and disseminate it can liberate our people.

That is one of the reasons why the Black Press of America, that coalition of black newspapers numbering little more than 200, is so vital. Not only have they consistently informed 15 million African Americans about the local, state, regional, national and international issues that affect all of us, they have simply told our story like it needed to be told. But let me add a dose of reality in this: black newspapers have got to get off their duff and put into place the needed quality and substance that Black America deserves. I'm sorry, folks, but there are some black newspapers nationwide that are terrible. These newspaper owners do a severe injustice to the legacy of black newspapers from the past by offering an inferior product and then demanding that black folks pay for it. In age where desktop publishing, digital cameras and

120

Speak, Brother!

inexpensive software can allow anyone to produce a slick, comprehensive and manageable product, there is no excuse for what we see each week. Folks, spell check is as easy as clicking a button. Like it not, that is the truth.

Now I know some of you are sitting there and saying, "Who does he think he is to take off on black newspapers, black radio and black television?" I'll tell you who I am: I'm the former managing editor of two of the top black newspapers in the country that have won a ton of awards for journalistic excellence; I'm the former news director and morning anchor of a black radio station; I've produced for a black television network; I provide news reports for two radio networks that target black folks; I'm the news editor of a national black magazine; I'm the editor of a black website that is founded by the number one black morning show personality in the country, Tom Joyner. I can easily work for any of the major newspapers in this country. Yes, I have the skills and the journalistic awards to get a job at the *New York Times*, the *Washington Post* or the *LA Times*. But I choose not to. I choose to forgo a paycheck from a mainstream operation to do exactly what I want to do. I don't have to ask anyone whether I can write a story or go cover a trial here or a convention there.

By working for the black press and having the access to the same individuals as the Associated Press, ABC, CBS, NBC and CNN, I can tell *our* story when it is being distorted through someone else's lenses. And that's why there is an inherent danger is us not owning us because when it's time to give the black perspective, the decision to run it may come through the lenses of someone with blue eyes. Don't get me wrong, there are white and Hispanic brothers and sisters who have more of a conscious that many of our brothers and sisters whose skin has been kissed by nature's sun. But we know by history that we can't depend on anyone else to do for us than us.

See, there comes a time and point when people of righteousness must stand up and say what needs to be said. No longer can we afford to sit on the sidelines and allow the madness to continue. No one – and I mean no one – can tell our story, or as the owners of the first black newspaper said, "plead out cause." Only we can do that.

Now you may be asking, what does that have to do with me? I'm not a journalist. I don't work in a newsroom. I can't interview the president. Good question. And the answer is simple: get up and do something. Make a personal decision that you will no longer sit back and tolerate such misinformation and ignorance to run rampant throughout this industry. You cannot save the world on your back. And don't take that attitude because it will only discourage you. But make the decision to speak out and say, "I disagree with that and I'm going to let someone know." Call the news director. Call the editor. Write a letter. Send an email. Let your voice be heard. Just as our brothers and sisters decided to sit at the counter and demand that they be served, you must have the same diligence and demand that you be heard.

Speak, Brother!

Who can forget the action a few years ago of a dentist in Fort Worth who was so fed up with the negative images, cursing and nudity on television that he began to write advertisers. His actions, coupled with signing up a few supporters, brought many television networks to their knees. Why? Because without advertising, no newspaper, radio station, TV station or website can survive. That is the lifeblood of any media institution.

But you can also make the decision that if your children, nieces or nephew are going to watch television, make sure they are going to watch something that invigorates their mind, body and soul, and not some mindless and soulless video or sitcom. For every 30 minutes of the *Wayans Brothers*, we should mandate that twice as much time be spent watching other fare. As a child I read some 300 books each summer. If your child, or for that matter yourself, is engrossed in comic books or shooting a basketball, make the point of saying, "Let's make a deal. For every one of those you will read two of these." I had this conversation the other day with my barber. He has chosen to help his son develop his basketball skills. Every time I see Cotton with his son, his son is bouncing a basketball. I don't begrudge that, but when I see Cotton's son, I ask, "Are you reading?" And I must give Cotton some credit, this brother didn't get mad at me for asking that question; he embraced it and even humbled himself by saying that he wasn't doing his job and was letting his son down by not emphasizing reading *along* with his basketball development. Now how do I serve as a living witness? Every time I get in that chair to get my haircut there is a book, magazine or newspaper in my hand. I'm constantly feeding my mind because I have the chance to spread that knowledge via radio, TV or the Internet.

You can do the same. You can increase your knowledge. You can take advantage of what is offered to you and what sits before you. The television and radio doesn't have to be reduced to an idiot box. It can be uplifted to be tool to expand knowledge.

But the greatest question is: What are you prepared to do? Are you prepared to step up and make your voice heard? Are you willing to put yourself on the line? I know I am. If you're not, don't worry. Just get the hell out of the way and allow those of us who are willing to liberate Black America through the mass media go down that road.

Diverse voices to be stifled by continuing media consolidation

March 11, 2002

Mega media companies like AOL Time Warner, Viacom, Clear Channel Communications and Disney are salivating at the opportunity to become even larger behemoths after a recent decision by the U.S. Court of Appeals to throw out long-standing rules dealing with ownership of media properties.

The court threw out the Federal Communications Commission ban on a media company owning a local television station and cable outlet in the same market. Although they didn't toss out the FCC's provision limiting one company from owning local television stations that reach more than 35 percent of the television viewing audience, the FCC was ordered to justify the provision or rewrite it.

Officials from the various companies say the rules are archaic; they even went as far as to say it was violating their First Amendment rights. Thank goodness the courts weren't duped into believing that nonsense. As expected, large media companies say deregulating gives the consumer more options and is better in the long run. But that logic is nonsensical, silly and downright wrong.

Ever since President Bill Clinton signed into law the Telecommunications Act of 1996, the communications industry has been turned upside down. Large companies, backed by billions of dollars from major banks, went nuts and began to snap up anything they could find: billboard companies, radio and television stations, and other media properties.

Take for instance Tom Hicks. The Dallas investor had never before owned a radio station, yet when the caps were lifted, he quickly built one of the largest radio station ownership groups in the world. Why? Not because he loved radio, but because he knew he could cash out by flipping the company. He eventually sold the stations to Clear Channel, now the largest radio owner in the country (also the largest billboard owner).

A result of the media swapping and buying has been a tremendous loss of jobs, a lack of creativity and diversity in ownership and a movement by a handful of media companies to own nearly everything. That means the big boys who are able to throw millions at a company and walk away with a basket full of properties shut out committed folks who want to grab their piece of the pie. It isn't surprising that there has been a dramatic decrease in the already low number of African Americans and other minorities who own media properties.

It is troubling when Viacom is allowed to own a major network affiliate and a UPN station in the same market, known as a duopoly. What that has caused is a combining of staffs with one general manager and news director responsible for both operations. That's a loss of jobs and more people in the

Speak, Brother!

unemployment lines. But Wall Street loves to see these kinds of cuts because it increases shareholder value and allows companies to meet their 20 percent to 30 percent annual rate of return.

The merging, swapping and buying of properties also means that the media companies will use their largeness to bully other media entities to do things their way. For example, Disney has been frequently accused of playing rough with cable operators by saying that if they don't carry and pay increased subscriber fees for what seems like a dozen ESPN networks, ABC Family and the other networks they own, they will pull them from the cable company. AOL Time Warner, the nation's largest cable operator, has also been accused of using their power to force cable networks to fall to their knees and accept their demands. In business it's called tough negotiating, but what it also does is freeze out the small players from getting their networks on the cable system.

Wall Street and corporate execs say, "Bigger is better." But that thinking is an absolute farce. And it is one that has become like a virus in many of America's industries such as banking, oil and gas, auto and technology. What media "bigness" causes is one company being able to go to advertisers and offer them deep discounts by bundling several companies, thereby causing smaller operations to fail in landing major advertising contracts.

This is not a sexy issue that people can rally around. It pales next to racial profiling, vouchers and the many other substantive issues we read about every day. But it has lasting ramifications because if a chosen few began to own everything, our news and content will look remarkably similar (is it me or does every radio station sound the same?) and diverse voices will be left on the side for the sake of profits.

In America we call this capitalism. I say it's just plain wrong.

Write your member of Congress. Send e-mails to the FCC and the White House.

By remaining silent you essentially give tacit approval to what is taking place. And when we don't see diverse reporting and television shows, we'll all wish we had spoken up when we had the chance.

Don't hide behind First Amendment
when ignorance is to blame

Jan. 27, 2002

Let me get this out right now: As a man who made the decision to become a journalist at the age of 13, I have spent 20 years defending the rights of journalists and the protection the U.S. Constitution affords a free press.

I am equally a proud 1991 graduate of Texas A&M University, a school where I earned my journalism degree and one that allowed me the opportunity to learn so many new and exciting things and meet a host of people from all racial backgrounds.

But there is no way my love for the university, nor my passion for journalism, will allow me to defend the racially insensitive editorial cartoon that recently ran in the school newspaper, *The Battalion*.

If you haven't been following this mushrooming story, *The Battalion's* editorial cartoonist, who calls himself "The Uncartoonist," ran an editorial cartoon that the paper's editor said was trying to emphasize staying in school and getting good grades.

I have absolutely no problem there. The two characters – a young man and his mother – were drawn as having dark skin. Again, no problem as far as I'm concerned. But where the issue met major resistance was in the use of stereotypical images that have been used to demean blacks since the 1800s: bugged eyes, large noses and big lips of the characters.

The editor of *The Battalion* said he saw the editorial cartoon and thought there wouldn't be a problem with it. But that statement is just another example of how out of touch some people are with reality.

The African American Student Coalition has called for *The Battalion* to issue an apology for the racially insensitive cartoon. The school's president, Dr. Ray Bowen, issued a stern rebuke of the paper, and others have heaped criticism on them as well, including head football coach R.C. Slocum (it seems this episode hasn't helped with the recruiting of talented black prospects).

The paper has so far refused to apologize, instead printing an editorial saying it was all a misunderstanding and calling for campus town hall meetings to discuss the racial climate at the university.

Some have said that this whole episode has been a huge learning opportunity for the student editor, fellow staffers and students in general. The eternal optimists say the university newspaper is a laboratory where students can get a taste of the real world and learn from their mistakes.

Oh how right they have been.

Ever since this story became public, campus officials have been deluged with inquiries from members of the media, as close as Houston and as far

125

Speak, Brother!

away as New York. On Monday, the heat will get turned up when the angered students will hold a campus rally, which will include representatives from the Houston branch of the NAACP.

There is a lot to say about youthful indiscretion and making decisions without understanding the full ramifications. And yes, we are talking about students and not professionals. But as a member of the media for 12 years, I have witnessed professional journalists make decisions just like these students did. I can recount first hand in radio, television and newspaper newsrooms the kind of backwards decision-making that has resulted in similar outcries, and have also seen editor's retreat behind the First Amendment just like these students are doing now. The last thing I want to see are insensitive and racially ignorant editors at school newspapers today becoming tomorrow's publishers, editors and news directors. We can ill afford to have another generation of journalists who "just don't get it."

The editor at *The Battalion* is Hispanic, and he says he's on the side of the black students. But I don't care if he was midnight black, what we don't need in this business are people who are clueless about such issues.

I have heard people say that the black students are being thin-skinned and they saw nothing wrong with the editorial. But unless you have been on the receiving end of such racist attacks you would never understand.

Despite what The Uncartoonist said, this is not an attempt to make the newspaper politically correct. This is the attempt to stop decades of racial stereotyping that has only divided this country. These images were the mainstay of the Jim Crow movement, which only ended in the 1960s. Many of the college students today are the offspring of those who were born in those tumultuous times.

A large part of the problem stems from the fact that so many students, and a ton of adults, refuse to acknowledge past racial issues and have no historical context. They may see something as cute or funny and not even remotely consider how it may be felt by someone else.

Officials with *The Battalion* should apologize. Instead of defending ignorance, they should accept their medicine and truly use this as a learning experience. Texas A&M University Department of Journalism officials should incorporate diversity and racial and gender sensitivity into their classes and curriculum in order to fully examine the effects of such decision-making. They should make the effort to bring in a variety of minority journalists to provide seminars and workshops to the students so they can hear what's it's like in real newsrooms.

And if they don't? Then *The Battalion* workers will continue to live in a cave and hide behind the First Amendment, while the protesters exercise their First Amendment rights and continue to protest. You can bet that I'll be with the latter group.

American media deserve to wear a scarlet 'O.J.'

Oct. 8, 1994

As self-appointed protectors of free speech and the First Amendment, we in the media fiercely defend our right to stick out noses, as well as note pads, cameras and tape recorders, into someone else's life.

And although there is a tremendous need in a democratic society for a press not shackled by a paranoid government, there comes a point at which we in the media must put aside our grandstanding in favor of common decency and respect.

My occasional embarrassment with my peers has only been compounded by the reckless and mindless behavior that has been seen since Hall of Famer O.J. Simpson slowly rolled down a Los Angeles freeway in the back seat of white Ford Bronco with a gun to his head.

With each passing day, the public has been inundated with information regarding the case, much of it wrong.

At first we heard, according to confidential sources close to the case in the police department, the medical examiner's office or the district attorney's office, of the finding of a bloody ski mask or a bloody weapon that looked like a military knife or tool. But the "evidence" never existed.

And days before the selection of a jury that will decide whether Simpson will return to his Brentwood mansion or spend the reset of his life in prison, Los Angeles TV station KNBC, on the basis of information from "confidential sources," reported last week that DNA tests showed that Nicole Simpson's blood had been found on socks recovered at her former husband's home.

Attorneys on both sides blasted this report, which the station later retracted. It caused Judge Lance Ito to criticize the report and consider not letting cameras into the courtroom.

The media, whether it's the *Los Angeles Times*, the *National Enquirer*, CBS or *Hard Copy*, have elevated this case to unbelievable proportions. We've seen local newspapers and TB stations set up their own jury pools, legal teams and hordes of talking heads to give their "expert" opinion on the evidence or what the next move will be for either side.

But what is the point of all of this? Perspective?

One argument presented by the media has been that we are only feeding a hungry audience that has been startled, mesmerized and gripped by the case of a former football start-turned-actor accused of killing his former wife and her friend.

But that is not sound journalism. It's an attempt to get larger ratings and sell more newspapers. We are the same as the shameless vendors outside of the courthouse in Los Angeles hawking "Free O.J." buttons, shirts and other mementos.

Speak, Brother!

And in the face of this insanity, I have been both saddened and angered by the deafening silence from the leaders in the journalism industry.

Where are the presidents of the Freedom Forum, the Society of Professional Journalists, the National Association of Broadcasters, the American Society of Newspaper Editors, the Newspaper Association of America and the Radio Television News Directors Association?

They are sitting on the sideline as the people they supposedly lead and represent run amok. They should be demanding that reporters, editors and news directors show some restraint and moral leadership in the face of the madness.

So the next time someone attacks the media for being inaccurate, perhaps we should consider the Simpson debacle.

Our critics may be more correct than we think.

Burning desire to get a story leaves privacy in ashes

Aug. 19, 1994

As friends and family members of Emmett "Pete" Allen slowly walked down the steps of New Rising Star Missionary Baptist Church on Saturday, newspaper and television photographers recorded each tear, every sad expression and the moving reactions of the stricken family.

But as Allen's 78-year-old mother, leaning on a friend, slowly moved toward the awaiting limousine, a television photographer darted past her in a mad dash across the church's lawn, pointing his camera toward another church exit.

As a number of the 900 mourners frantically looked to see what the commotion was about, five other photographers raced to the side of the church, all in an attempt to capture a picture of the devastated nephew of Allen, and the son of his confessed killer.

And while my peers nearly slammed their lenses against the window of the car in which Oliver Miller Jr. was riding, I watched and heard many of those people who came to pay their last respects to Allen say that my colleagues looked like cockroaches when the kitchen light is turned on.

It was certainly my most embarrassing moment as a member of the media.

When covering tragedies such as the killing of a respected community leader, the aftermath of a tornado or hurricane, we are always cautioned to think about the people we are questioning rather than editors and news directors who have made it clear that we should get the story.

Yet we don't always do that.

Too often I see reporters berating people, hurling questions at them in an effort to force them to answer us. But the question we never seem to ask is: "How much can we gain from this?"

It was a shock to us in the media, as it was to the Allen family, to find out that Oliver Miller Sr. confessed to killing Emmett Allen.

But as Isadore Edwards Jr., pastor of New Rising Star, pointed out during his eulogy, the younger Miller must carry a burden many us have never experienced: the idea that a man who served as a big brother to you died at the hands of your father.

And it was against that backdrop that many of the cameras were fixated on the 24-year-old, a center for the National Basketball Association's Phoenix Suns.

We were all waiting to see Miller's reaction and maybe get a quote or two from him. But the young man, who didn't even enter the church until near the end of the service, refused to comment and tried to shield himself from the cameras while sitting in the car.

Speak, Brother!

The younger Miller was definitely a *part* of the story, but he was not *the* story. It was clear to all that he was not commenting and wished not to be bothered. But instead of shooting from a distance, we ignored his wishes and intruded on his privacy.

The Allen family let us be there to record, for history's sake, the turnout at Allen's funeral and the kind words being said about him. But we should have been more conscientious of the grieving family.

The funeral of a loved one is a private moment to be respected.

I believe in a free press, but I also believe in a responsible one. We are continually asked to live up to a high degree of professionalism when doing stories, but we also must have a sense of sound moral judgment and basic respect.

We just forgot that we were only guests at Allen's funeral.

The story doesn't have to be sacrificed in an effort to accommodate the family. There are always ways to tell a story without being intrusive. The question is: Do we want to make that extra effort?

Diversity in the news media remains an elusive goal

July 29, 1994

As I stood at the copy machine the other day, I glanced through the window into the editorial conference room and shook my head.

As the editors from all departments of the *Fort Worth Star-Telegram* met to decide what was going to be in the next day's newspaper, it was disheartening to not see an African-American, Hispanic, Asian American or American Indian at the table.

It is a story I'm sure will be told many times by my colleagues who are in Atlanta this week for the first joint convention among the nation's four minority journalism organizations.

The event, billed as Unity '94, was expected to attract more than 5,000 students and professionals who will network, attend professional development sessions, discuss problems and, more importantly, devise solutions to meet the need for diversity.

A number of critics – including many minority journalists – question the gathering of the National Association of Black Journalists, the National Association of Hispanic Journalists, the Asian-American Journalists Association and the Native American Journalists Association. Some chose not to attend, suggesting that the organizations should not unite with anyone until they are individually unified.

But the problems that minority journalists and their respective communities face daily are more important than the minute reasons of those who opposed a unified convention.

The continual negative coverage of minority communities and the lack of recruitment and retention of minority journalists are two issues that are foremost in the minds of us all.

When the Kerner Commission, appointed by President Lyndon Johnson to investigate the causes of the 1960s race riots, told the country's leaders that there are two Americas – one black, one white – many finally began to see what African-Americans and others had already known.

In that report, the media were taken to task because of the lack of minority journalists. The report concluded that lack of diversity contributed to one-sided and poor reporting on riots and their causes.

Since then, there has been a push by media organizations, both large and small, to bring more of "us" in as reporters and at the executive level. But although numbers today exceed those of 20 years ago, we are still playing catch-up.

The four minority journalist conventions have given media managers in large and small towns a chance to meet minority journalists, talk with them and, in many cases, hire them. But they have also served as an opportunity for

131

Speak, Brother!

white managers, many not fully understanding the problems faced by minority journalists, to get a firsthand look at our fears and frustrations.

It is very difficult for people to understand how it feels when you are the only African-American or Hispanic in a newsroom, and you are constantly slamming up against managers who are not receptive to your ideas and suggestions, whether they involve story ideas or recruitment.

Many minority journalists grow weary and leave.

During the last year, minority and white staffers, as well as members of the African-American community, have raised the issue of a diverse staff with the editors and executives at the *Star-Telegram.*

These concerns are not new, but we have received a commitment from management to aggressively recruit more editors and reporters and improve our coverage of ethnic concerns.

We sent a contingent of people to the convention to recruit, and we plan to blanket the job fair and hotels with our job listings. But that is the first step. We must continue this process year-round and make sure that we are attracting and retaining the best talent in the country.

When I'm feeling down and burned out, all I have to do is remember that conference room and realize that all of us still have a lot of work to complete.

SECTION SEVEN
GENERAL

Speak, Brother!

Divorce can't kill God's greatest gift

June 6, 1999

A year ago next month I was sitting in a Washington, C.D. airport restaurant, waiting on a flight to my home in the Dallas-Fort Worth area.

I was wolfing down a hamburger and fries with a friend as our plane was readied, and the issue of marriage and divorce came up. It was a sensitive issue for him, a prominent journalist, because he had recently gone through a tumultuous divorce that ended a 20-year marriage. Like many people who are the major wage earner, he talked about losing many of the assets accrued during the marriage: a significant art collection, house, cars and a load of money.

"I'll never get married again," he said. "I'm not going through this again."

His pain was evident. The sense of agony was real. Not just over losing his precious collection, but also having to accept no longer being with the one woman he committed himself to. It wasn't a feeling that I wanted to ever be able to share with him.

Unfortunately, I can no longer say that.

In about three weeks my marriage will come to an end. Almost six years and three months to the day since were stood at the altar at St. Mary's Cathedral in Austin (March 27) and made a covenant between the two of us and God, we will stand before a judge who will deliver the news that the marriage has been dissolved in the eyes of the law.

Even thinking about it doesn't feel good.

This wasn't the plan. When I packed my stuff in Dallas, leaving behind friends, a job I loved, lots of money and other opportunities to return to my hometown where my wife had taken a job, this wasn't on the radar screen.

The thoughts of grandeur were evident: Me, managing editor of the city's top Black newspaper where I first got my chance to write nine years ago. She, Debra Duncan, as in the popular host of the *Debra Duncan Show* on Ch. 13. We made for one of those "power couples." A shining example to Black couples and others that two people who are on the fast track are able to cope with the "instant friends" who seek you because of your status; lots of money; and the stress of difficult jobs, and still have a loving and committed relationship.

But those visions became blurred and wiped out with three words, "I want out." Problems were evident for a while and both parties were equally at fault. But the commitment was made by both parties to do everything humanly possible to make it work. But I guess the commitment wasn't as firm as I thought.

We can spend a lot of time pretending that getting divorced is a simple task. We see the billboards across town that say, "Divorce for under $100." We

Speak, Brother!

read the books on how to get divorced or download the paperwork ourselves from the Internet.

Friends and family of both parties say, "You better get yours" or "I didn't like her anyway" or "I'm glad you ditched him." But the pain is real, and as Dennis Rainey, executive director of FamilyLife, an Arkansas group that focuses on building marriages said, "divorce is a living rejection."

For many of us the marriage covenant is real. Saying those words isn't just an exercise; it is a real and honest commitment. I don't believe in staying in a marriage if someone is beating you and sexually assaulting you or any other acts of violence. But with other problems, such as lack of communication or selfishness, we are quick to run out the back door and not face our own issues when it comes to marriage.

We as a society have accepted the notion that if you have a few dollars in the bank, friends on the side who you spend time with, and a roof over your head, then you are better off without the other person. But what we are sometimes saying is, "I'm not willing to work and compromise and forgive."

So we get divorced. It's an exercise that has been explained as being easy. But it's not. You think about the friends you lose. The first kiss. The first time you made love. The last time you made love. The memories you shared. The lost moments. The money you saved and now stand to lose. And what it feels like to really have someone say, "I don't want you anymore."

We don't like it when an employer says your services are no longer needed. We didn't like it when a boyfriend or girlfriend in high school calls it quits. So why should we fool ourselves into thinking that divorce will roll off our backs and life will be so much easier tomorrow?

I've come to the conclusion through my experience and talking to others over the years that we run from what is difficult. Having to look yourself in the mirror and address your issues as they relate to someone else is difficult. It's hard to admit that we have a selfish attitude that prevents us from sharing all that we have with someone else. It's painful to admit that because our mother and father didn't show affection to us as children we don't know how to be intimate with our husband or wife. It's demoralizing to admit that a failure to have material goods as a child makes us seekers of fame and fortune as an adult. It's difficult to admit that having a sibling get all the attention when we were younger causes us to crave attention when we are older. And it's tough to admit that seeing a mother or father not openly and lovingly praise their spouse has made us oblivious to our spouses winning awards or using their talents to make crafts around the house.

We can brood or get divorced when faced with these difficulties, or we can do what has always worked: Pray. That's right, pray.

Stormie Omartian, in the awesome book, *The Power of a Praying Wife*, tells women (and men, this can and should be applied to you as well!) to stop complaining and not forgiving and "shut up and pray."

Speak, Brother!

It's amazing how we have the belief that God can raise the dead, heal us from terminal illnesses and bless us financially, yet he can't restore the peace, love and happiness in a relationship and marriage. But just like when it comes to an illness, we have to believe with all our hearts that he will grant us favor on our marriages.

If you read the comments from the couples we interviewed for this week's cover story, the most consistent thing they said was that a family that prays together stays together. No, not the wife going to church while the husband is at home. No, not the husband praying in one room while the wife is off at the office during another 18-hour workday.

We all must understand that evil forces seek to break apart what God has put together. That was in the marriage vows, remember? Those forces don't come into your life and say, "Hey! I'm here to tear this apart!" But they do come in the form of friends, family, job and money.

Any couple who is married or anyone considering taking that walk must understand that marriage isn't any relationship. It is *the* relationship. It must be taken seriously by committed people.

Thankfully, through the power of prayer, I'm not bitter at the concept of marriage and hate every woman who walks near me. Some people have that feeling after they've been rejected. Surprisingly to some, I'm even more committed to marriage than I have ever been. That's not need talking. Instead, it's my word to God that I'm going to be the man he made in the likeness of Him.

Do I still love my wife? Yes. Am I still committed to the marriage? Yes. Even if she tells me five minutes before the papers are signed that she wants to work it out, I must honor my covenant with God to do that. Nothing big or small, no friend or foe, can or should get in the way of that covenant.

Divorce is a wretched affair I don't wish on anyone. But as stated in Matthew 19:11-12 (Eugene Peterson's *The Message* translation), "Not everyone is mature enough to live a married life. It requires a certain aptitude and grace. Marriage isn't for everyone...But if you're capable of growing into the largeness of marriage, do it."

137

Daddies need love, too

June 10, 2002

If you took a poll and asked most Americans to name the top five holidays, I would be willing to wager $100 that Father's Day wouldn't be one of them.

My gut tells me that Christmas, Thanksgiving, Easter, Mother's Day and Valentine's Day would be ranked ahead of Father's Day.

For some reason we are a society that doesn't think fathers deserve the same recognition as mothers. I know, I know. Mothers have such a special relationship with their children. When Mother's Day rolls around in May, children make a concerted effort to get home, buy gifts or call mom.

But wait until June when Father's Day is upon us. There is absolutely no sense of urgency. Have you said or heard any of these lately: "Just get him something. He'll be happy." "I was just home last month for Mother's Day. You want me to come back twice in two months?" "Dad? Heck, a tie will do."

It has always been fascinating to witness the complete blow-off father's get. Need I remind the world that were it not for dad, mom could not have conceived the child? He does have a little something to do with the process!

Maybe the problem stems from dads just going on about their business and not seeking recognition. They just sit there, smile, read the paper, watch the news, tinker in the garage and keep on truckin'.

Comedian Chris Rock talked about this in his HBO comedy special, *Bigger and Blacker*. Rock said dads take care of business, but get no love. Dad always tells the kids to tell mommy that dinner was good or that she looks wonderful or congratulations on a job promotion. Yet dad gets a cursory thanks for what he does each day for keeping food on the table or making sure the lights stay on.

It amazes me to watch athletes on television who look into the camera and say, "Hi, mom." I'm like, "What's up with that?!" You don't believe me? Just watch the NBA draft. We get to see the athlete, his agent and mom. If dad is there, he doesn't even get a screen credit. No offense, but for a lot of folks, mom wasn't running around chasing a ball or teaching you how to tackle. Daddy was being the drill sergeant.

But to be fair, fathers have a lot to do with this as well. An increasing number of women are impregnated by men who then disappear, sometimes reemerging sporadically over the life of a child. In the black community, single moms head a pathetic 70 percent of households. I'm not calling the moms pathetic; it's the no-good, trifling men who are man enough for 15 minutes of sex but not 18 years of life. White, black or brown: you are a sorry excuse for a man if you get a woman pregnant and aren't responsible enough to help raise and nurture the child. You may not get along with mom, but that child needs you in their life.

139

Speak, Brother!

Single moms – and single dads – have done an awesome job of raising their children. But I'm a firm believer that a child is better off being raised by two loving parents – a man and a woman – than one.

I guess I'm a little sensitive on this issue because I've always had my dad. For 35 years he's been married to my mom and has always taken care of his family. He hasn't been the missing link in our family, nor does he spend time away from his family by hanging out with the boys or leaving home because of a mid-life crisis. He's been there physically, financially and emotionally (Although I wish he had left the house for a bit when I did something bad that resulted in getting my butt whipped! You're supposed to laugh at that one, dad).

It may be too late for this year, but I would hope all Americans would make a concerted effort to show dad a little more love and affection. And by all means, don't get him another damn tie. He may say he likes it, but he would have liked to have that spa treatment you gave mom last month.

True confessions needed for Catholic Church

April 19, 2002

"Therefore, O house of Israel, I will judge you, each one according to his ways, declares the Sovereign Lord. Repent! Turn away from all your offenses; then sin will not be your downfall. Rid yourselves of all the offenses that you have committed, and get a new heart and a new spirit." Ezekial 18:30-32, NIV

The act of confession is one of the most treasured rituals of the Catholic Church.

The church routinely emphasizes to its members to maintain a regular schedule of confession by going to their priest, spilling out their sins and allow the priest to counsel and bless them in order that their soul will be cleansed. I should know: 25 of my 33 years in this world were spent as a practicing Catholic.

But with each passing day bringing more devastating news of priests in dioceses across the country sexually assaulting innocent boys and girls, as well as the church covering it up, now is the time for the Catholic Church to do what it has been preaching.

Catholic bishops, who are essentially the chief executive officers of the individual dioceses, are certainly afraid of lawsuits and bad publicity by these issues becoming public. But the acts of these priests, some dating back decades, are illegal. They are not just immoral acts and sins against God but actions that go against the laws of the land. And by the Catholic Church covering them up by doling out millions in settlements to the abused, they are just as guilty of obstructing justice.

What is even more amazing is the lack of widespread condemnation and action from law enforcement and political officials after the sexual assaults became public. Yes, district attorneys in some cities are demanding the list of priests who have been accused of sexual assault, but every attorney general in affected states, and even the Justice Department, should be launching inquiries into what has taken place all of these years. The hypocrisy is even more significant considering the Catholic Church has taken a hard stance over the years on abortion, homosexuality and the death penalty, yet inside of its own house it has been harboring bonified criminals.

The nation has been outraged in the past over sexual and financial indiscretions of television ministers and others, but those pale in comparison to this sordid story.

It is distressing to read each story because it goes to the heart of what a person of the cloth is supposed to uphold: trust and integrity.

Priests, ministers and deacons have the respect and admiration of their congregations who entrust them with the welfare of their children. They are

Speak, Brother!

looked upon as spiritual leaders who chose a life committed to shepherding God's children. What moral authority does any Catholic priest or bishop have by standing in the pulpit and preaching about sin when they themselves have committed such egregious sins? We all sin and have fallen short of the glory of God, yet 1 Timothy 2 says that the overseer of the church is supposed to be above reproach. Clearly, Catholic leaders have skipped over that part of scripture.

We should feel sorry that these priests have fallen so deeply into sin and pray that God extends grace and mercy on them. But that should not remove the anger over the failure of church leaders to stamp out such sexual abuse and turn these sexual predators over to law enforcement authorities. Sending them to counseling is one thing; having the issue properly adjudicated is another.

The process has and will be a painful one. But that's what happens when you have done wrong and now are held responsible. It can't be done with a few simple statements from the pope or resignations from a number of priests. This ordeal is necessary to require a thorough cleansing of the church so that the stench is removed and the public can be reassured that all has been done to make sure it doesn't happen again.

Church leaders have been humbled by the vastness of the problem. But until leaders in each diocese purge their rolls of these sexual predators and make a public confession to atone for the past and pledge to operate fully and openly, they will not have the right to speak out morally.

Job said what happens in darkness will be brought to light. Now is the time for stadium lights to be shone on the Catholic Church.

Black and proud to be a graduate of Texas A&M

Feb. 26, 2002

I am a 33-year-old black man who grew up in a black neighborhood and attended mostly all-black primary and secondary schools. I am a member of a black church, a black fraternity, news editor of a black national magazine and editor of a black Web site that is owned by a man who is the biggest black name in syndicated radio, Tom Joyner.

That said, I am proud as hell to let anyone know that I am a 1991 graduate of Texas A&M University. Such a declaration may come as a surprise to some who have established a view that the university is not a welcome place for a person of color.

A recent report conducted by the university said as much, as well as the fervor surrounding an editorial cartoon that many, including myself, found to be racist, insensitive and downright wrong. The aftermath of the cartoon has produced a flurry of condemnation from black and other minority students, who have accused some on the campus of being negative toward people of color and fostering an atmosphere of hate.

At the same time, the defenders of the status quo have assumed a "take-it-or-leave-it" attitude, or as said in Aggieland to anyone who dissents from popular opinion, "Highway 6 runs both ways."

You will never see me defend any racist or insensitive practice by anyone. My love for the university will not overshadow the anger at seeing the bad decisions made by the newspaper in running the editorial cartoon. I have conveyed those concerns to the editor. But for better or worse, college campuses have never been devoid of the same maladies that affect society.

Just as civil protests have struck cities such as Miami, Los Angeles and Chicago, the same has happened at Penn State, Michigan, the University of Texas and Texas A&M. Are there racists at all of these colleges? Yes. Are there individuals who, despite being at an educational institution, don't take the time to expand their borders and learn about other cultures? Absolutely.

Why? Because the students are no different than their parents, grandparents and friends who have ignored people of color and have taken the view that "their issues" don't concern them. Despite Texas A&M being overwhelmingly white, it is not a "white university." As I explained to many of my fellow students at Yates High School when I graduated in 1987, "my parents and ancestors have been paying tax dollars to the university for years, so therefore, this is my damn school." That same mantra was repeated to several white students when I arrived on the campus to join my brother, class of 1990. (My sister is class of 1993.)

From the moment I stepped onto the campus during a visit to see my brother, I fell in love with its beauty and the friendliness of the student body.

143

Speak, Brother!

And despite what some black students have said, I love the traditions and camaraderie of the university. Did I participate in every tradition? No. But I will not say they are "for white people." I enjoyed them thoroughly and no one can argue with my black credentials.

I will never forget visiting Washington, D.C., as a freshman and heading to the Ford Theatre to pick up some tickets to the play *Elmer Gantry*. I happened to recognize a distinct ring being worn on the hand of an elderly white gentleman at the counter who appeared to be in his late 60s or early 70s. I asked him what class he graduated from and he told me 1940-something. He then inquired about the three of us who were there, all black men who were graduates or worked at the university. After chatting a bit, he invited us back to his hotel room to join his family-several of his children were Aggie graduates-to have a few drinks and talk "Aggie bull."

Imagine the scene: Three young black men and this elder white guy bound by one thing – Texas A&M University.

I have experienced that kind of reaction on countless occasions. At that moment, I realized what my brother had been telling me for a year: "This Aggie thing is real."

Texas A&M is a wonderful place to learn, meet new and exciting people and forge relationships that can last a lifetime. Is it for everybody? No.

But if a black man from an all-black world can grow to love Aggieland, then surely others – white or black – can open themselves up and expand their horizons. They will be better for it.

Jefferson-Hemings: The legacy of slavery continues

May 6, 2002

The decision by the white descendants of Thomas Jefferson to not acknowledge or accept the descendants of his black lover, Sally Hemings, only goes to show that decades and generations may have passed, but the refusal of white slave owners to acknowledge their black offspring continues.

The issue was supposed to have been settled in 1998 when DNA tests were conducted to show that one of Hemings' children did have the DNA of Jefferson. Even the Thomas Jefferson Foundation, which runs the plantation he owned, Monticello, agreed that Jefferson likely fathered Hemings' six children.

But refusing to admit the truth, the Monticello Association members formed their own scholarly panel to conclude that it could not have been Jefferson but maybe one of his brothers who slept with Hemings.

In a 24-page report, the Monticello Membership Advisory Committee report ruled that a "lack of universally acceptable information" prevents the Hemings family from joining with the 700-plus descendants of Jefferson and his wife, Martha.

One of the white family members, appearing on NBC's *Today* show after the vote, even went as far as saying that if the Hemings family is able to produce records or proof that the two were involved, they would accept that. He said that shouldn't have been a problem because the Jefferson slaves were allowed to read and write and should have relied on written documents instead of the oral word. Now isn't that amazing? Blame the slave for Jefferson cheating on Martha.

The contentious issue became even more interesting to me after spending some time with my grandmother, Emelda Lemond, this past weekend. She may be 81-years-old, but her mind is like an elephant's when it comes to our family history.

Mother, as we affectionately call her, was answering my questions concerning my late grandfather's relatives who migrated from Haiti to southern Louisiana. When asked about my great-grandmother, Mother said that she was the product of a well-known white doctor in Louisiana who slept with her mother and fathered two children. He didn't mind my great-grandmother assuming his last name, but wouldn't allow her brother to assume his last name. Why? Because he would have had rights to property in the largely patriarchal society.

Looking at the skin tone of my grandmother, grandfather and their daughter, my mother, it's not hard to figure out that somebody white chose to sleep with one of my ancestors. Such was the indignity of slavery and segregation: slave

Speak, Brother!

owners and bosses working the help in the fields and in the home, but also in the bedroom.

Thankfully, we are able to pull birth records to prove that the doctor fathered the children, but the descendants of Hemings don't have that luxury because slaves were forbidden from reading and writing and government agencies didn't keep any data on slaves.

Some may think this is a moot issue and that the Hemings family should drop it and move on. I disagree.

It is always the hope and aspiration of most folks to know where they came from and who their ancestors are. It's always a joy to be able to pull out albums that are stuffed with photos, documents and other items to share with our children in order to give them a perspective of their lineage.

I am the official photographer in my family and I do everything in my power to photograph and videotape all of our family events so I will be able to show my children, and they can show their children, who poppy, granny and Uncle Bubby were.

Unfortunately for many African Americans, we don't enjoy the luxury whites have of tracing their family roots back centuries and across the Atlantic. Knowing from whence you came is important in passing on a rich history to the next generation, but America's atrocious history of slavery will never allow that to happen for people of color.

The Hemings family says a vote to exclude them will not prevent them from telling the truth about their great-great-grandmother and great-great-grandfather.

Thomas Jefferson is considered one of the fathers of this country. Now it's time for the white Jeffersons to finally admit that he's the father of Sally's children.

Ain't no future in yo' frontin'

I've always gotten a huge laugh out of folks who are more concerned with showing the world they are a shot caller-big baller rather than actually being a shot caller-big baller.

You know who they are and what they look like. They are the folks who roll into a club and buy bottle of champagne, knowing full well they will have to beg for overtime to make up for it. They drop names of someone famous as if they are best buds, but in actuality, they were in the same room with them – along with 1,000 other people. They also may have a higher car note than their monthly mortgage. In the words of Joshua Smith, CEO of the Maxima Corp., "their assets are on their ass."

The constant need to buy things they can't afford just to impress people who don't like them anyway is an amazing character trait of far too many people.

This came to light recently when a young cat, after seeing my two-pager, remarked to a friend: "Oh, he has the baby two-way." His sorrowful look and condescending voice really ticked me off.

If you don't know, there are two kinds of two-way pagers out there: one is a smaller version that looks like a normal pager and allows you to send and receive e-mail. The other two-way is fairly large, has more options and is a lot more expensive.

I had to ask homey, "Did you pay for yours or do you have to turn it in when you lose your job?" (Sorry, a bruh couldn't help but toss that one out considering so many people rely on their jobs for cool toys, front like it's their own, but lose them when they are given a pink slip).

He continued to talk more smack, but then let this slip out, "Well, I haven't paid mine in three months."

Now how dumb is that? Here he is acting like he is the man, frontin' with his two-way on his hip, only to let loose that he hasn't paid it in three months. It got me to thinking about so many folks who do the same. Isn't it amazing so many of us talk about keeping it real yet we are leading fake lives?

While we sometimes get huge laughs out of this, it really is an issue that has larger ramifications because they strike at the heart of the lack of self-esteem and the need to prove to others that they belong.

Because of a variety of issues, many people in this world – and we know how it is in black America – are overspending like mad in order to keep up with, as your mama and daddy used to say, "the Joneses."

Some of us have been blessed with a nice, three-bedroom house, yet far too many of us work like mad and ignore our families in order to buy a larger house in a better neighborhood. The car we have runs well, but the Mercedes, Jaguar and Beamer is what we desire to have. So what do we do? We

147

Speak, Brother!

overextend ourselves, get financing on a huge bill and force ourselves to work harder in order to meet our monthly needs. I wonder: how much of our monthly income is being put in savings? Are we even tithing that 10 percent? How much more is going to a college fund?

What is happening is that we accrue more and more debt, get a second or third job to pay for these items, but continue to buy more and spend more, which in turn keeps the cycle of financial ruin in perpetual motion.

Again, this is not an indictment on everyone, but there comes a time and a point when we have to stop the madness, step back and say, "Enough! I'm going to be happy and content with what I have a live a satisfied life."

I know that may sound like a novel idea and some may find it's too hard to do, but I think not. It's a matter of reaching a point where we are comfortable with our lives and ourselves.

Contentment is a state of mind that goes against the grain, but it sure makes life a heckuva lot better. It really comes down to continuing to strive for the "good things" in life without sacrificing what is most important: God and family. For those of you who fit the mold of wearing the designer labels from Needless Markup and sporting the $300 pair of shades just to name drop its maker, give it up. It does nothing to make you a better man or woman.

There is nothing more appealing than meeting someone who walks with an air of confidence in their entire being. Those folks allow their spirit and nature to speak for them, as opposed to relying on material goods to convey their true essence.

Let's make it a mission to chill with the frontin' and work on building our self-confidence by relying on what's on the inside instead of gaudy and expensive toys and labels on the outside.

I Am Somebody! 'Cause I've got security

Sept. 11, 2001

"I got no posse. No bodyguard. Hell, I ain't no senator. What I need bodyguards for? I tell jokes." Bernie Mac, Savoy Magazine, October 2001

A few years ago, a friend of mine was asked during Super Bowl week her impressions of all the hoopla. Always one with an acerbic tongue, she quipped: "I've never seen so many has-beens with security in my life."

It used to be common for presidents, prime ministers and other elected officials to be led and followed by a contingent of people with wires sticking out of their ears, dark shades, bulges on their hips and dead serious looks on their face that simply said: "Don't even think about it."

But those days are gone. Nowadays, the sons and daughters of famous folks drop by restaurants and bars with a big beefcake clearing the walkway and demanding special treatment. It has gotten to the point where it's laughable to see the lengths that some folks have gone with the "security detail."

No industry is worse than those in the entertainment field. You go to a charity benefit, concert or grand opening of a nightspot and someone walks up with eight or 10 members of their entourage and walk into a joint as if they are the President and First Lady. It seems as if there are more bodyguards at the Emmys or the Academy Awards than you would find at the White House.

Every year at the Kentucky Derby, where the truly rich folks hang out, there is an annual joke among the bluebloods to see which used-to-be-all-that actor or actress comes trekking through with their bodyguard and the invisible leave-me-alone sign on their face.

You can't even speak to some people for fear of ticking off the mindless bonehead who is protecting them. But the question I always have is, "Who are you protecting them from"?

Yes, there are some nuts out there in this celebrity-crazed society that stalk entertainers, send unsolicited love letters and dang near attack them.

Michael Jordan needs to be flanked to get to his car from the gym. Tiger walks the course with an assigned officer, not just for crowed control but also for constant death threats. Earlier this year, the FBI uncovered a plot to kidnap actor Russell Crowe. I understood why he was heavily flanked at the Oscars. But there is such a thing as overkill.

And I knew the love affair with the pomp and circumstance that comes with security and the entourages had reached the extremes when I dropped by a church in Dallas three months ago to listen to Bishop Eddie L. Long speak at a conference.

After Long concluded his sermon, I walked "backstage" – folks use concert lingo even for church hallways these days as a way of keeping the have nots

149

Speak, Brother!

away – to say hello to the bishop. I wasn't some stranger looking to pull at his coattails: during a stint in Atlanta last year, I attended his church for three months, bought a ton of tapes and books, and had just recently profiled him in *Savoy* Magazine (Style and Substance, June/July 2001).

My progress towards Long was stopped by a brother who declared the hallway adjacent to the pulpit was "a secured area" and I needed "clearance" to be back there. I couldn't help but laugh, especially considering I have been "cleared" for 12 years by the United States Secret Service on any number of occasions – which includes a full background check – as well being in the inner sanctum of Nation of Islam leader Louis Farrakhan (his security detail, the Fruit of Islam, is second only to the Secret Service when it comes to being on alert).

After much wrangling, I was asked to step outside the hallway and wait until I was cleared by his security detail (he actually didn't travel with bodyguards; it was local folks assigned to be with him). Nearly 20 minutes passed as I waited along with my wife, an ordained minister who was none too pleased with the shenanigans. All I could do was laugh at the brothers with their wires sticking out of their ears, holding people at bay and getting a lift from their personal power trip.

Tired of waiting, I finally opened the doors and walked towards the room Long was waiting in. I overhead the bishop say, "Guys, all I want to do is speak to the man who just wrote a story on me." There seemed to be a logjam as 20 or so people stood around, bewildered as to what to do about this request. Gospel singer Daryl Coley even had to step in and say, "Guys, the bishop has asked to see this man. Let him in." Finally, we got a chance to speak.

It took all of this nonsense for me to approach a minister to say a quick hello. I couldn't help but remember how easy it was for folks to approach Jesus.

We have reached a point in society where far too many people have been mesmerized by the energy created when an entourage shows up; it somehow lends legitimacy and power to the individual. Singer, actor, minister, comedian or elected official, the lifestyles of "famous folk" has somehow changed the morals and values others have lived by all of these years.

I can understand security for the minister who is getting death threats for striking out at drug dealers. But I can't understand the minister who, while preaching, has his security detail slide along the walls, following his every step as if he were the president. I don't understand why a singer without a hit to his or her name has to have four brothers push through crowds to get inside of a club. It's hard to fathom six security guards ordering people away from The Rock, the WWF wrestler, when just a few feet away stands the head of the Democratic National Committee, a man who sits at the feet of the president. Is something wrong with this picture?

150

Speak, Brother!

There are so many things in life that we can love and cherish about celebrities. But folks, let's kick to the curb the foolishness of the power trippin' personal assistant, the diva moments of a R&B star without a single Grammy to her name and the unnecessary police force known as someone's posse. It's not cute; it's not necessary; and frankly, I'm not impressed.

Ain't nothing like black-on-black love

Sept. 6, 2001

Over the last few days my e-mail system has been inundated with notes from folks around the globe who wanted to show their appreciation for my column on Aaliyah and the criticism her funeral received from a *New York Post* columnist.

Although responding to the 300-plus e-mails will be hard – I promise to try – I can't help but smile and laugh when I see comments like Larry Bonner's "awesome response" or Doris Franklin of Gastonia, North Carolina, writing, "bravo, bravo." And I can't forget Shanela Brackins "you go boy."

The response made me think of a comment made last week by Tom Joyner, who is founder of BlackAmericaWeb.com and who does a little radio show you might have heard of. He talked about the response the morning crew gets when they visit various cities and the e-mails and phone calls that come in daily.

"People approach us like we are family," he said, noting that fans remember the day they previously met them down to the clothes they had on.

Two months ago while speaking at the NAACP convention, I recall Tavis Smiley saying the same thing as he reflected on his feelings after being terminated from BET. Although he has certainly landed on his feet – five jobs, a ton of money and more exposure – Smiley said he had never experienced such a feeling of warmth and appreciation from an adoring public.

I can never get enough of attending the annual National Association of Black Journalists convention, where I get to see so many friends, colleagues and comrades in this struggle we face each day. A hug from Pat Tobin, a slap upside the head from Sheila Brooks or an always-funny joke from Vernon Jarrett is a guarantee.

It's never beyond me when my friend and former colleague here in Dallas, Sherilyn Smith, is always there when I need her the most: when I'm out of town, she volunteers to check the mail or deposit a badly needed check or even scoop a bruh when he needs a ride from the airport.

And my feelings cannot reflect the love I remember from the 1995 Million Man March; seeing so many smiling brothers hugging, embracing and speaking to one another was an awesome feeling. Every time I watch Spike Lee's *Get on the Bus* tears stream down my face, not because of what was said on that day, but really about the tremendous love from a collective body.

I guess in telling all of these vignettes I'm trying to suggest that there is something deeply special about black-on-black love. It's hard to describe it without someone actually experiencing it.

That's why it pains me considerably when I see the brutal tongue lashing that goes on between brothers and sisters in various venues across the country.

Speak, Brother!

I can't fathom a black man laying his hands in an aggressive fashion on a black woman; going toe to toe with a fellow brother over a simple misunderstanding goes beyond my thought process; seeing an abandoned baby left in a dumpster is unthinkable; or seeing black folks jump all over a black director because all characters aren't positive in an upcoming movie about police brutality.

We have gone through so much hell and catch enough hell that the last thing we need from one another is to add more trash to the heap that seems as if it will overwhelm and cover us up completely. Maybe we have had so much abandonment and hold on to so many bitter feelings – beatings and rapes at the hands of white slave masters, daddy leaving and never coming home or our sisters getting pregnant and never going to college – that love is the last thing we want to give because we are so fearful of being hurt. Again.

There is no single human being who can wrap his or her arms around all of the brothers and sisters in this world and give them a group hug. There is no one black newspaper, website, radio show or television network that can tell every story and always be positive. But as individuals, we can make a concerted effort, even when we may not feel up to it, to say, "Hello, how are you doing, brother?" to the cat that is checking our luggage at the airport. Will it pain us to read the name tag of the sister behind the counter at the drug store where we get our paper and coffee and say, "Dottie, how is your day going?" I don't think our fast-paced world will somehow come to a screeching halt if we see a great story on television and we get the phone book, call the station and leave a voicemail for the brother and sister and say, "Hey, just wanted to tell you that I loved that story and you are appreciated."

I have learned from personal experience that you might just be an angel from heaven someone person needed to get through their day or week. It is my hope that each and every one of you will make a conscious effort to speak, hug, kiss, acknowledge, congratulate, emulate and stimulate a fellow brother or sister.

'Cause if you've ever done it or experienced it, there ain't nothing like black-on-black love. Trust me, you'll be better for it.

Thank God for the Mama Baileys of the world

April 26, 2002

When kids are asked who do they want to most be like when they grow up, the usual names are rattled off: Oprah Winfrey, Bill Gates, the President of the United States, Michael Jordan or Tiger Woods.

We never hear a child say, "I want to be like Mama Bailey."

I first came across this wonderful woman of God several weeks ago while visiting Inspiring Body of Christ in Dallas. The Rev. Rickie Rush, the pastor of the church, recognized Mama Bailey as the church's Member of the Year.

It was fascinating to find out what made this woman so special that the pastor would choose her out of nearly 5,000 members and recognize her on this day. It didn't take me long to figure out why it was such a no-brainer.

Mama Bailey is not a woman who runs a big-time corporation in the city. She doesn't walk around exerting her influence on public policy, on a first name basis with the mayor and a few members of Congress or discovering great things in a medical lab. She is simply one of those discreet and silent saints who goes about her business by helping so many people through the difficult moments of life.

Rev. Rush told the congregation that Mama Bailey doesn't even own a car and rarely has money in her pocket, yet whenever there is a member of the church in the hospital, he says he will get there and find she is already there holding their hand and praying with them. When his own mother died, Mama Bailey didn't even ask anyone whether his father needed help, she just went over and cooked him several meals and sat on the front porch, tending to his needs while he grieved over the loss of his wife. It was by her presence and giving spirit that his father finally came to church, something even the pastor couldn't get him to do!

One woman stood up and said that when she lost her child through a miscarriage, she and her husband were distraught and didn't know what to do. Yet there was Mama Bailey, offering them a shoulder to cry on and providing them with comforting words and prayer.

And as these nice things were being said about her, Mama Bailey lay spread out on the altar, prostrating herself before the Lord and giving him thanks for the gifts being bestowed upon her, including money, a TV/VCR, a shopping spree at a store and other goodies.

What was evident by the story of Mama Bailey wasn't all the great things she did. It was the simple fact that she lived a prosperous life because she availed herself to the Lord and chose to do his will. Rush said Bailey, who was retired, never fretted about money or a car or a big house. All she cared about was going where God sent her and doing what he commanded of her.

155

Speak, Brother!

Again, the material goods didn't matter; it was her spirit that was rich and priceless.

If any of us ever wonder what it means to be spiritually prosperous all we have to do is think of Mama Bailey and her work for the Lord. It truly is more important than much of what many of us are driving ourselves to accomplish.

Discrimination is the wrong way to empower women

Dec. 26, 1994

When Gen. Earl Rudder decreed in 1963 that women would be admitted into Texas A&M University, the vehement protests from military corridors and bases across the world swamped switchboards at the state's first public institution of higher learning.

Women, except when they remained in subservient roles and "stayed in their place," were considered the evil enemy to men at the then-military institution and would destroy the many traditions honed since the school opened its doors in 1876.

Yet even then, women could only be admitted into the school if no other state-supported schools offered the course of study, if they were enrolled in graduate programs, or if they were the wife or daughter of an enrolled student, faculty or staff member, according to a 1988 issue of *Texas A&M Today*.

The restrictions were lifted in 1971, and women were admitted on a basis equal to that of men.

But since Rudder's controversial decision 31 years ago, the university has grown from a small school in the sticks of College Station to one of the world's finest.

And women certainly have played a significant role in the development of the former Agriculture and Mechanical College of Texas.

So it was with regret when I witnessed the scowls, taunts, vicious signs and diatribes from supposedly educated students, faculty and staff members at Denton's Texas Woman's University who protested its regents' vote to allow men to be admitted to the institution's undergraduate programs.

Ever since the board voted 6-1 on December 10 to admit men – the school only allows men into its nursing and graduate programs – students at the country's largest university for women have assailed administrators for turning their backs on the predominantly female student body.

Yet in all the talk and media attention swirling on the 270-acre campus, I have yet to hear an accurate, honest and convincing argument as to why men should not be allowed to attain a degree from an institution that receives 58 percent of its budget from the state.

I've heard students and faculty say that the mission of the school – to empower women – will be destroyed when those hairy, sports-minded, sex-crazed maniacs flock to the campus.

But here is one reason why the board of regents, looking to avoid a costly lawsuit, made the decision: discrimination.

It is downright sexist, discriminatory and unlawful for any public institution to deny the rights of an individual based on gender.

Speak, Brother!

Women and feminist groups, namely the National Organization of Women, have been fighting officials at Virginia Military Institute and The Citadel for years to allow women into those bastions of male supremacy.

Their arguments? It's wrong to deny women entrance to schools that receive state funding. Sound familiar?

Men at those schools have been saying that their traditions will be destroyed and their mission irreparably harmed. Sound familiar?

Prairie View A&M University and Texas Southern University are the state's two historically African-American public institutions, yet those schools are open to non-blacks.

The two schools still maintain their mission as a mecca of African-American higher learning, but officials there always understood that it was racist to not admit whites or anyone else who wanted to get a public education.

If women at Texas Woman's University want to go to an all-female school, they should dig deep into their pockets and transfer to Smith, Vassar or Mount Holyoke.

Before the women at TWU leave their college careers behind and go into the real world, they must understand that the future of our society rests on people of all races, colors and genders being given an equitable chance, especially in the public domain.

There's no better place to learn that valuable lesson than in a place of higher learning.

Education has been trumpeted as the answer to discrimination and sexist attitudes. It should not be a place where sanctioned ignorance is allowed to continue.

Teachers need praise – not criticism

December 1996

With December upon us, now is the time to get ready for Christmas, check our gift lists two or three times, and for us early birds, to figure out how much dough we have to give Uncle Sam in the form of taxes.

But this month, I am particularly happy for one reason: the end of the fall semester.

When my college career came to an end in December 1991, I vowed never to return to the classroom unless it was a speaking engagement. But somehow, I actually agreed to accept an adjunct teaching assignment at the University of Texas at Arlington this semester. I knew what kind of student I was and the thought of facing someone like me was not a good one. But I chose to teach anyhow.

And what a surprise that lay ahead for me!

Grading papers, dealing with the multitude of excuses from whiny students and seeing the posturing and political maneuvering among them was a hilarious, yet informative exercise.

But being on the other side of the podium did allow me to have an impact on the minds of our future workers and to teach them the inner-workings of journalism. It also gave me the chance to gain a measure of respect for what teachers endure each and every day.

There was always a saying among my relatives when I was young that if you didn't make it in your chosen career field, you could always work at the post office or become a teacher. While the former may sound easy, my work over the last four months will never cause me to suggest the latter is an easy task.

Elementary, middle and senior high schools, along with college instructors, are truly the backbone of our society. I have always felt this way, but it has become so much clearer since I began to have to take roll, dole out assignments and do the other responsibilities that come along with the job.

It takes a truly special person to know how to handle 38 different egos, problems and personalities. Whether it's the student who wants an excused absence for wanting to attend a sorority event to the student who has failed tests but needs a B to stay in school or to the student who is shedding tears because she won't make an A, a teacher must know how to balance all of those individual needs in the pursuit of education.

Yet the job of a teacher must also be to stay tough and rigid while making exceptions for moral reasons. It is easy to remain hard and fast by applying the rules evenly, but that is not reality. We are all human and that human mindset always comes into play.

Speak, Brother!

There have been many teachers over the years that have made statements that have destroyed the psyche of students.

"You're nothing." "You'll never make it." "You shouldn't do that."

But there have been so many more who have made lasting impressions on many of us.

The job of a teacher goes beyond grading tests and giving lectures. It is also about teaching kids and young adults about responsibility, fairness and equality. That may sound mightily righteous to some, but it's true.

It would be easy for me to tell one of my students to go shove it and deal with every grade they've earned. But I've also got to tell that student what he or she needs to hear to continue striving to be the best and not to give up. My goal is not to destroy their dreams and aspirations but to give them the mental edge to deal with adversity and the pitfalls they will face upon graduation.

I often look back on my school days and am appreciative for the many words of wisdom – some quite stern – that made me grow up and accept my responsibilities. All of the heartache and trouble I got myself into was worth it in the end because it forced me to deal with reality and accept my own faults.

Teachers will never be paid along the same lone as entertainers, athletes or movie stars; yet their impact on our lives is much greater than that of Emmett Smith, Michael Jackson or Denzel Washington.

Those who reside in the classroom are often blamed for many of the problems of our society, but they shouldn't be because many of them are doing the best they can.

Now is not the time to criticize our teachers for what they are doing. Instead, we should be praising them for being caring enough to withstand all the pressure we place on them for the pittance they are being paid.

So the next time you see a former teacher who taught you, don't walk past them and not speak. Just say thanks for being there and making you a better person. They need our support and prayers.

ABOUT THE AUTHOR

Roland S. Martin is a nationally award-winning journalist and editor of BlackAmericaWeb.com, the black news and information site founded by nationally syndicated radio show host Tom Joyner.

He is also the news editor for *Savoy* Magazine, a New York-based national lifestyles magazine targeting African Americans. Mr. Martin is also a correspondent for the American Urban Radio Network. His weekly column is also distributed to newspapers across the country by Creators Syndicate.

He has also written for several national media outlets, including Honey Magazine, Impact247.com, Savoymag.com, Inside.com, NiaOnline.com and Netnoir.com. Mr. Martin also produced an election special for Major Broadcasting Cable Network in Atlanta, Georgia. He also is frequently called upon as a content and marketing consultant for a variety of media outlets.

Mr. Martin has interviewed a number of luminaries, including President George Bush; Vice President Al Gore; Texas Governors Ann Richards and George W. Bush; a host of members of Congress; the Rev. Jesse Jackson; Barbara Jordan; Supreme Court Justice Clarence Thomas; former U.S. Ambassador Andrew Young; and athletes and entertainers such as Michael Jordan, Dr. J, Tiger Woods, Erykah Badu, Kirk Franklin, and Vivica A. Fox.

Martin is a member of the National Association of Black Journalists, Alpha Phi Alpha Fraternity, Inc., and is one of 32 national Unity Journalists of Color mentors.

The 1991 graduate of Texas A&M University is married to the Rev. Jacquie Hood-Martin and resides in the Dallas suburb of Cedar Hill.

He can be reached via e-mail at roland@rolandsmartin.com. For more information, go to his website, www.rolandsmartin.com.

ORDER FORM
Speak, Brother!
A Black Man's View of America
BY ROLAND S. MARTIN
You can order online at
www.rolandsmartin.com

Shipping Information:

Your name:

_____

Address:

_____

City: _____ State: _____ Zip code: _____

Telephone:_____E-mail: _____

Price schedule:
1-4 books: $9.95 each
5-9 books: $8.95 (10% off)
10-24 books: $8.45 (15% off)

25-99 books: $7.95 (20% off)
100+ books: $6.95 (30% off)

Your order:
Number of books _____
x price per book _____ =

_____

Sales tax for books shipped to Texas address
Only (Add 83 cents on $9.95 or 8.25%)*

_____

Shipping is $3.50 for one book;
$1 for each additional book

_____

Total cost

_____

Make checks payable to Martin Media Group. Shipping charges for orders of 10 or more is less than calculated. Please call (972) 293-8374 or e-mail roland@rolandsmartin.com for exact charge. Allow three weeks for delivery.

ORDER FORM
Speak, Brother!
A Black Man's View of America
BY ROLAND S. MARTIN
You can order online at
www.rolandsmartin.com

Shipping Information:

Your name:
_____

Address:
_____
_____

City: _____ State: _____ Zip code: _____

Telephone:_____E-mail: _____

Price schedule:
1-4 books: $9.95 each   25-99 books: $7.95 (20% off)
5-9 books: $8.95 (10% off)   100+ books: $6.95 (30% off)
10-24 books: $8.45 (15% off)

Your order:
Number of books _____
x price per book _____ =

_____

Sales tax for books shipped to Texas address
Only (Add 83 cents on $9.95 or 8.25%)*

_____

Shipping is $3.50 for one book;
$1 for each additional book

_____

Total cost

_____

Make checks payable to Martin Media Group. Shipping charges for orders of 10 or more is less than calculated. Please call (972) 293-8374 or e-mail roland@rolandsmartin.com for exact charge. Allow three weeks for delivery.